The Entrepreneur's Survival Guide

Tips and tricks to help you start and build your company

Based on compilation of articles from
"Leading Your Company: Real Solutions"

Mark Paul

Second edition
Fourth printing - 2011

The Entrepreneur's Survival Guide

Tips and tricks to help entrepreneurs start and build their companies.

Abstract: If you are an entrepreneur who is starting, thinking of starting a company, or looking to take your existing company to its next several levels, this guide is a must read. It can save you years of learning the hard way and help you turbo-charge the start-up & ramp-up process. The principles explained in this guide are presented in a quick-to-read series of topics ranging from getting a new company off the ground to improving marketing and sales performance, as well as operational, and project performance.

Paul, Mark
> The Entrepreneur's Survival Guide
> Second edition, fourth printing
> © 1998-2001, 2003, 2007, 2010-2011 Mark Paul
> All rights Reserved
> ISBN 0-9708665-2-6 / EAN: 978-0-9708665-2-3

The Entrepreneur's Survival Guide
Tips and tricks to help you start and build your company

Table of Contents

Forward   v

Introduction   ix

Preface   xi

Executive Summaries   xv

Section 1)   Leadership Effectiveness

- What Makes a Great Leader?   3
- Are You Ready for Your Next Level?   9
- What are the Core Values of Leading CEOs?   15
- A Simple Secret to Successful Leadership   21
- Change Leadership: Taking Your
  Company to New Heights   25
- Your Leadership Style: Inspiring Followership   29
- How to Bankrupt Your Company
  Without Really Trying   33
- Develop Your Strategic Plan in Two Days   39

Section 2)   Building Your Company

- How to Build Your Company   45
- Raising Money in a Tight Market   51
- Building Your Game Plan   57
- Building Your Team   63
- Building Your Story   71
- Creating Your Stock Structure   75
- Building Credibility   81
- The Realities of Raising Money   85

Section 3) Improving Marketing and Sales Performance

- The Real Value of Market Research 91
- How to Value Price Your Products and Services 95
- Maximizing Marketing ROI: Research to Sales 101
- Strategic Selling Skills for Technology Entrepreneurs 107
- How to Attract Significantly More Customers 113

Section 4) Improving Operational Performance

- Organizing for the Customer 123
- Achieving Peak Company Performance 131
- How to Hire the Best People 137
- How to Predict the Future 145
- How to Manage Projects 149
- How to Define Products 159
- Solutions for this New Millennium 163
- Reasons Why Some Organizations Perform Poorly 171

Bonus Addenda

Can be found at www.synergy-usa.com/ESG-bonus.html

- Affinity Diagramming Defined
- Venture Teams Defined
- Program Management Glossary
- The "Physics" of Marketing
- Must-ask Questions, before you start

Acknowledgements 201

About the Author 207

The Entrepreneur's Survival Guide

Forward - Second Edition

Achieving entrepreneurial success is an awesome challenge –
somewhat akin to climbing Mt. Everest. This book can serve as
your wise and trusted "Sherpa" on this formidable journey. The
Guide distills an enormous amount of information, wit, and
wisdom into a highly readable digest for the entrepreneur.

Its snappy style will capture your attention and keep it focused on
straightforward and pragmatic concepts and activities. Mark's
thoughtful compilation will help you navigate the treacherous
waterways of new enterprises. If you want to start, grow, and
manage a new business, this book is a "must read."

The text is extremely well organized with thoughtful diagrams,
examples, checklists, and practical tools for the entrepreneur. In
addition to its comprehensive content, the material is organized so
that targeted chapters address specific issues or concerns.

Most importantly, this book does NOT make false assurances about
"success" factors in starting and building your own company.
Instead, Mark tries to help the creative entrepreneur identify and
formulate his or her own "special sauce."

I heartily recommend this book for those contemplating starting a
new company or business. Reading and referring to this book will
give you a head start on the road to success.

Debi Coleman, Managing Partner
SmartForest Ventures
Portland, Oregon

Forward - First Edition

Entrepreneurial experience is a key element to success. But experience is not a commodity and is very difficult to teach efficiently and pass along; it's like "capturing lightning in a bottle." Mark Paul has captured the "lightning in a bottle" that is the entrepreneurial experience. The Entrepreneur's Survival Guide methodically and effectively outlines the process of evaluating a business concept and bringing it to fruition as a new enterprise. I was amazed at how well the book captures the essence of the steps required to increase the chances of entrepreneurial success, yet is so easy to read and absolutely practical. This is a must read for those considering entrepreneurial pursuits.

Eric Pozzo, Vice President
Operations: First Silicon Solutions, Inc.
Board of Directors for ABC Technologies,
A serial entrepreneur.

Introduction

This book is not trying to be all things to all people. It is not a book on leadership effectiveness, though it has a leadership section. Nor is it about "management." It is about helping leaders develop their businesses. It is about entrepreneurship and about helping companies to outperform themselves.

Concepts on people skills, motivational techniques, and how to win friends and influence people are left to others. This book is written to help business owners and other company executive/leadership/management team members ask themselves difficult questions, the answers to which will help them overcome difficult situations. It is also intended to act as a reference guide, when the next step in a company's evolution places roadblocks in the way.

So enjoy the book for what it is – a compilation of "How to" articles, that also asks questions only *you* can answer - intended to help you get your companies to its next level.

Preface

When I landed my first job out of college, it only took a week or so to realize I was not prepared for the realities of the business world. Neither college professors nor any courses taught me to understand an organization chart so I could learn who to talk with – in order to solve specific problems or get a certain task completed. I didn't understand how customers' needs were identified, or how solutions were supplied within the company to satisfy these needs. There were no classes on how to start and effectively run a company, let alone successfully lead an organization to exceptional performance. Although that has certainly changed in the past couple decades – with many business schools and entrepreneurship centers providing excellent preparation for students – *real-world solutions to real-world challenges* are hard to find.

During eleven years at two Global 500 companies, I came to realize the best of the free enterprise system was also the worst: Freedom. Freedom to succeed, freedom to fail, freedom to have those individuals who could lead – rise to the top of the company. Larger companies have the resources to provide post-graduate training and education, but not all companies do. Therefore, the bulk of "fast-movers" are those who can rapidly learn from the mistakes of others and can understand and solve complex market, leadership, organizational, operational and project problems.

During my twenty-two years of consulting, I've seen recurring problems within start-ups and established companies alike. In a market-driven economy, those entrepreneurs who figure out it's "OK" to ask for outside assistance are the entrepreneurs who can morph their companies to meet ever-shifting market demands. Typically, entrepreneurs are ill prepared to tackle the very difficult challenges associated with starting and/or growing a company. In fact, entrepreneurs have trouble taking their companies to the next level because they have to deal with "classic" problems – problems which have been solved by others, before – yet persist in *their* company.

Based on over three decades of business development experience, I've concluded that new and experienced entrepreneurs alike need a "survival guide" on how to deal with the real-life issues others have faced and already solved. With this as a guiding light, I wrote a series of chapters to tackle tough challenges entrepreneurs face every day. This is not a book of answers: This guide asks questions. The answers are unique for every situation in which you may find yourself.

These chapters have been organized into "natural" sections, and are based on the successful first edition of The Entrepreneur's Survival Guide, first published in 2001:

- Leadership Effectiveness: Companies are built on the vision, values and drive of individuals. The most essential characteristics that make people great leaders can also be their biggest weaknesses. This section looks at how specific characteristics of leaders can be fine-tuned for greatest affect to build your company.

- Building Your Company: Fundamental actions executive officers can take to get their company on a firm foundation are discussed in this section. The tips and tricks in this guide are as important to existing companies as they are for entrepreneurs looking to form new companies.

- Improving Marketing and Sales Performance: Doing the necessary market research and determining the specific value you can offer your customers is discussed in this section.

  From customer research to maximizing revenue, this guide helps you determine if there is a "there", there and can set you up for success.

- <u>Improving Organizational Performance</u>: Strategic and tactical changes you can make that can turbo-charge your company are dealt with in this section. From project management to strategic planning, hiring the best, and improving organizational development.

Each section and chapter is meant to help entrepreneurs of small to medium sized companies – to provide advice and guidance from a practical perspective.

I hope to help entrepreneurs kick-start the progression to their next level. So please enjoy the suggestions in the light they were meant: to help your company outperform itself.

Mark Paul - Portland, Oregon - October, 2007

Since the original printing of the first edition of this book, several organizations have validated its use – implementing it to help entrepreneurs and business owners develop their companies:

⇨ MIT Enterprise Forum, Venture Labs
⇨ Oregon State University: Food Innovation Center
⇨ Oregon State University: Capstone Project (Dept. of Agricultural)
⇨ OTBC's "TechLaunch Bootcamp" & FastTrac® Series
⇨ Willamette University: Atkinson School
⇨ University of Oregon: Lundquist Center for Entrepreneurship

Through this book, I have been able to help thousands of people – I couldn't normally reach through consulting – start, build and grow their companies.

For this, I am very grateful.

Mark Paul - Portland, Oregon - June, 2011

Entrepreneur's Survival Guide
Tips and tricks to help you start and build your company

Executive Summaries

Section 1: Leadership Effectiveness

What Makes a Great Leader?
There are several characteristics that set you apart as the founder and leader that allow you to lead people to great accomplishments. An assessment of your style relative to these traits should reveal something about yourself: Are you balanced in these areas? Are there areas of weakness that need bolstering? Do you feel uncomfortable in your role? What are your strengths? There is no one right answer to these questions – your personal assessment might surprise you.

Are You Ready for Your Next Level?
Whether you are a first time entrepreneur or seasoned executive, taking your company to its next level can be a daunting experience. Serious self-assessment is needed before embarking on the journey. By asking yourself difficult questions, you will be better prepared to make the tough decisions required to propel yourself and your company forward.

What are the Core Values of Leading CEOs?
What do company leaders rank as their highest priorities in leading their company? What are Chief Executive Officers' core values? This chapter reveals what CEOs desire from their companies and provides insights into their thinking. Compare and contrast your own values against leaders in high-technology companies – to gain a better understanding of how to significantly improve your company's performance.

A Simple Secret to Successful Leadership
As founder, you know there are ways to both run and ruin your company. Sometimes, the line between these two outcomes is very thin indeed. However, through the use of one simple equation, you can dramatically increase your company's odds of succeeding.

Change Leadership: Taking Your Company to New Heights
Many change programs end in failure – not due to the improvements being brought in, but because of *how* changes are implemented within organizations. This chapter addresses the human side of change management – to bring lasting performance improvements to companies looking to accomplish aggressive goals.

Your Leadership Style: Inspiring Followership
At the end of the day, the entrepreneur has either led a team to accomplish very difficult objectives or not. Everyone knows when the company has exceeded everyone's expectations. And they know when this has not happened. The major questions are: How do you inspire people to follow you? How can they be so compelled to focus most of their personal and all of their professional efforts towards achieving a company's never-changing desire for growth and improvement, in an ever-changing world?

How to Bankrupt Your Company, Without Really Trying
Over and over again, companies make the same mistakes. Wouldn't be nice to have a list of those mistakes, which are the most costly to companies? This section summaries the errors and omissions leaders make. Fix them, and you stand to dramatically improve your company's performance!

Develop Your Strategic Plan in Two Days
How can you spend time on strategic planning when you have to respond to every customers' wishes, your bankers' request for last quarters' financials, and just making payroll? Now, in just two short days, you can develop sufficient planning to plot the future of your company in ways you never thought possible. Find out how!

Section 2: Building Your Company

How to Build Your Company
This chapter could as easily be placed in the Leadership section, because it discusses six key characteristics that leaders must have in order to build their company.

Raising Money in a Tight Market
Finding capital is even tougher now that the NASDAQ and DOW have seriously eaten into angel investors' funds. What can entrepreneurs do to find capital in a tight market? This chapter addresses key points to act on to improve your chances of funding.

Building Your Game Plan
So you think you've got a great new idea that will sell bazillions of new widgets, have 95% gross margin and blow away the competition! All you'll need is a couple hundred thousand dollars. Surprise... only a few percent of plans *actually get funded*. Why don't the rest? Several business aspects considered in this chapter *must* be considered when starting or building your company.

Building Your Team
Would you like to double revenue? Triple profits? Increase cash ten times? Your company can easily break through current performance and achieve the "next level."

Building Your Story
Are you a start-up entrepreneur who needs money? Are you asking, "Do you know where I can get to investors who will fund this idea?" There are several things you - as the leader - must do in order to convince investors to part with their money. Find out how to dramatically increase your chances of getting funded.

Creating Your Stock Structure
When looking for equity financing, entrepreneurs often ask me: *"How much of the company should I give up, and when?"*, *"What happens when I lose control?"*, *"How much will our stock be worth... and when?"* A well thought out business plan, with accompanying financials will answer

most of these questions. However, an often-overlooked piece of the puzzle is corporate stock structure, to create a clear road map for stockholders and to help guide your funding decisions.

Building Credibility

You've got a great idea but few, if any, customers. As the leader for a start-up company or if you are trying to take your company to its next level, you have plenty to worry about. If you aren't Steve Jobs or Bill Gates, and have an unproven concept, how do you get anyone to quickly buy in? How do you increase your chances of funding? How do you minimize the amount of the company you'll need to sell? If you are interested in learning how to dramatically increase the probability of getting funded, this chapter will help you get going.

The Realities of Raising Money

You have a great product idea, you've done market research - there's a huge demand for what you've developed, your business plan is done and you're ready to raise that $1.5 million so you can implement your plan. All you need now is to convince people how great your plan is! Here are the "usual suspects" to consider when trying to raise money.

Section 3: Improving Marketing and Sales Performance

The Real Value of Market Research

"We don't have time for market research! It costs too much, takes too long, and just confirms what we already know." Sound familiar? A fundamental understanding of your customers' needs is critical to what you offer, your corporate positioning and your marketing strategy. If fear of extinction doesn't motivate you to listen to your existing and potential customers, please don't read this chapter.

How to Value Price Your Products and Services

Would you like to determine how much your customers will pay for your new products *before* drafting your first design or spending your first development dollar? This chapter explains how you can understand your customers' specific needs and get the most money for your products and services.

Maximizing Marketing Return on Investment

How would you like to have a direct marketing response rate of 25%. A return on investment of over 40 to one? With the tips and tricks in this chapter, you can work your way through a process that will tie marketing with sales and dramatically increase your revenue!

Strategic Selling Skills for Technology Entrepreneurs

In today's high-speed, high technology business environment, many great new companies are built on ideas from technical people. However, many outstanding ideas never get to market, nor receive funding. Why? No real understanding or appreciation of the selling process. There are some fundamental things technically minded entrepreneurs can do to propel their company to its next level. Read how!

How to Attract Significantly More Customers

This chapter brings together several of the concepts discussed previously – to help entrepreneurs turbo-charge their customer-attraction process.

Section 4: Improving Operational Performance

Organizing for the Customer

Ever wonder how you can get your products and services to market faster than your competition - with features and performance so advanced your customers don't mind paying more for *your* solution? So do a lot of chief executives.

Achieving Peak Company Performance

Have you ever asked yourself "How can I turbo-charge my organization?" Or "How can I increase revenue without spending more money?" There are several ways for your organization to achieve superior performance, which are discussed in this chapter.

How to Hire the Best People

Have you ever had to let someone go because they didn't live up to your expectations? Or they turned out completely different from what their resume indicated? Or you got exactly what you wanted but not what you needed? If this sounds familiar, then you're not alone! There are several things you can do to improve your hiring results. Learn how in this chapter!

How to Predict the Future
With customers, markets, and competition changing all the time, it seems nearly impossible to stay ahead of the competition. If you'd like to make the best decisions and know the resulting outcome ahead of time, then read this chapter.

How to Manage Projects
Many clients have hired me to help them increase profits by improving their product development. Here are my secrets on how *not* to manage projects. By ignoring these seven critical product development areas, your company will better respond to the market and beat your competitors on price *and* schedule.

How to Define Products
The effect of slow time-to-market has a definite cause: poor product definition. To minimize the amount of time, cost and risk associated with getting products to market, entrepreneurs need to invest in clarifying the "fuzzy front end". To do otherwise will cause your company precious resources in restarts and lost opportunities.

Solutions for the Next Millennium
If you are interested in learning fundamental shifts in the new economy, and how to position your company's product development for the next millennium, then this chapter is a must-read!

Reasons Why Some Organizations Perform Poorly
Many change programs end in failure - not due to the improvements being brought in, but because of how changes are implemented within organizations. This chapter addresses the human side of change management - to bring lasting performance improvements to companies looking to accomplish aggressive goals.

Section 1

Leadership Effectiveness

- **What Makes a Great Leader?**
- **Are You Ready for Your Next Level?**
- **What are the Core Values of Leading CEOs?**
- **A Simple Secret to Successful Leadership**
- **Change Leadership: Taking Your Company to New Heights**
- **Your Leadership Style: Inspiring Followership**
- **How to Bankrupt your Company Without Really Trying**
- **Develop Your Strategic Plan in Two Days**

The purpose of this section is to deal with first things first. Without leadership & high-quality, timely decision-making, the senior executive team will be forever mired in the minutia that *is* managing a company. With any organization, people look for leadership. They want to know someone has core values they can rely on, and a vision and mission they can support. Leadership is truly a balancing act: Balancing the need to successfully implement a well thought out plan, while remaining flexible to changing market conditions, balancing corporate objectives with personal objectives, and balancing customer satisfaction while growing profits. These are just a few of the daily decisions leaders face. Although this section focuses on the CEO, the ideas and lessons presented are true for any current and/or future entrepreneur, or "CXO".

What Makes a Great Leader?

Whether you are leading a small project, starting a company, or running a 30-year old, $300 million a year business, as the Chief Executive Officer, several characteristics set you apart. These attributes allow you to lead people to great accomplishments. A close assessment of the personal traits described below should reveal something about yourself: Are you balanced in these areas? Are there areas of weakness that need bolstering? Do you feel uncomfortable with some traits but not others? There is no one right answer to these questions. However, a better understanding of personal dynamics may make you an even better leader.

Developing leadership traits takes time; sometimes years. Some CEOs feel uncomfortable in their position, usually because the demands placed on them may run counter to their basic nature. If you do not naturally enjoy talking to large groups, you will have trouble holding company-wide meetings, or communicating with the press. If your vision or direction is unclear, people will have trouble following you. If you are highly flexible, employees may feel you are inconsistent in your demands on them. To better prepare yourself for continuing your journey as CEO and taking your company to even greater heights, take a moment to see where your strengths lie, and determine how you can best use these strengths to lead your company.

Personable: The ability to foster follower-ship is at the essence of leadership. This is reflected in the CEO's ability to talk with people at their level, take positive steps to praise and congratulate employees in public, be easy to work with and for, motivate employees to exceptional personal performance, and celebrate projects' successes. It also manifests itself in the ability to listen and be a team player. Leaders put people before goals by showing generosity and compassion.

There are two other very important people-oriented characteristics:

✓ **Communicates well**: Being able to clearly and concisely communicate your ideas and vision, both in writing and verbally, helps stakeholders appreciate and understand CEOs.

✓ **Encourages leadership:** Someone who allows employees to occasionally fail encourages risk-taking and ensures their people are skilled in handling even more difficult challenges in the future.

Entrepreneurial: Good leaders are entrepreneurs, in that they are *visionary*, or able to see things others cannot; *future-focused* by striving to actually change the future; *optimistic* in believing that their actions will make a difference; *risk-takers* in thinking that the rewards will outweigh potential negatives; *persistent* in trying to always win, no matter the personal sacrifices; and *growth-oriented* in knowing that they are building on prior wins and losses. Entrepreneurs are driven by:

✓ **A desire to improve the world:** At their core, leaders desire to make the world a better place. This desire may be seen in their sense of community, in their hope to increase people's standard of living or solve a significant societal problem, or in their desire to make a difference at a fundamental level.

Whether it is by inventing computer peripherals for handicapped people, making our lives easier by automating repetitive daily tasks, speeding up telecommunications, solving energy problems or creating new vaccines, the entrepreneurial spirit reigns supreme in CEOs.

✓ **Unreasonable Expectations:** In addition to wanting to improve the world, CEOs tend to have unreasonable expectations about several things. They are time-obsessed, impatient, somewhat paranoid, highly competitive, and early adopters of innovations. They expect others to quickly grasp their intuitions and can easily become frustrated when others do not. A common saying rings true, "Reasonable people adapt to their environment. Unreasonable people expect their environment to adapt to them. Therefore, all change – and therefore progress – is driven by unreasonable people." It is having that Big Audacious Goal that sets leaders apart.

Strong character: Leaders by their very nature have strong character. They tend to be charismatic so people want to follow them, dynamic in their actions as well as words, and uncompromising in their fundamental beliefs and desires. They strive for excellence in themselves and their team, and have a bias for action – to achieve significant results in a short time. CEOs also exhibit these characteristics:

✓ **Positive:** CEOs see humor in situations, and generally have fun. They are generally positive in their attitude and take a "can-do" approach when confronted by problems.

✓ **Ethical:** Great leaders are honest in their dealings with people, and do what they say they're going to do. They follow through with their promises and look for ways to create win/win situations.

✓ **Works hard:** Chief executives are task-focused, with an intense attitude about success. They are tenacious and purposeful in completing projects and are generally workaholics, driven by their own standards of excellence. They are energetic beyond their years.

✓ **Demands Excellence:** Demanding excellence in themselves and others also sets leaders apart.

Business acumen: Great leaders have a professional and exceptional understanding of business. They are business-like in their dealings, competent at handling complex situations, exceptional at decision-making thought processes, financially astute, highly competitive, and are thoroughly professional managers. They are profit oriented and understand how to make a profit, while appreciating the process and striving for outstanding results. Leaders are organized, taking time to think through challenges, and planning ahead. They are situational in their dealings with people and projects, cost-conscious, aggressive in setting achievable goals and reaching them, driven to meet commitments, and able to quickly initiate damage control when necessary. They are also pragmatic, customer-focused, and strategic in their thinking. They take a "50,000 foot view" when plotting a course and a ground-level view when implementing it.

✓ **Knows what is important:** By being situational, leaders can grasp or create the big picture and then can effectively communicate the smallest details to others, be they board of directors, team members, the press or investors.

✓ **Experienced:** Exceptional leaders are experienced. Which reminds me of the saying, "Good judgement comes from experience. Experience comes from poor judgement." This is why boards of directors search for seasoned professionals to take control of floundering companies.

✓ **Tactician:** Great CEOs can also be individual contributors when necessary, and can get in the trenches to complete projects or close sales.

Intelligent: What also makes leaders stand out is that they tend to be intelligent *and* street smart; technically astute, especially in technology-enabled companies; and often wise beyond their years.

✓ **Creative Problem-solver**: Leaders are intuitive, creative, analytical, leading edge, outside-the-box thinkers.

Good gut feel: Balancing out all the characteristics of a leader, is gut feel. At the end of the day, after all the team-oriented problem solving and analysis, decisions have to be made. A great leader generally makes the right decision, based on the facts *and* based on gut-feel. Good gut feel comes from great intuition, being insightful about challenges, and seeing things others cannot.

Is it possible that there are leaders who exhibit these traits day in and day out? Probably not. Every person and company has their ups and downs. However, successful leaders have these characteristics within them.

By having your vision, sharing your vision, building your team, instilling loyalty, and gathering and applying the resources to accomplish your dream, you will be in a position to help your company outperform itself. When everyone works towards the same goal, amazing things can happen.

Are You Ready for Your Next Level?

Whether you are a first time entrepreneur, a 'serial entrepreneur' or seasoned CEO, taking your company to its next level can be a daunting experience. So much so, that a serious self-assessment is needed before embarking on the journey. By asking yourself a few questions, you will be better prepared to make the tough decisions required to propel yourself and your company forward.

What do you really want?

Before embarking on a new venture or working to build your existing company, what exactly are you looking for at a personal level? A bigger challenge? More money? Excitement? A need to create a better tomorrow? To elegantly solve a significant societal problem? Meet your own and your investors' return on investment targets? In order to set up yourself and your company for success, it is important for you to answer these questions and know what is driving you. It is your specific motivation that will carry you through to your objectives.

✓ **For the first time entrepreneur**: Saying you want to grow fast and return huge sums to your investors, when all you really want is a nice-sized paycheck, has built-in conflicts that will make it very hard to achieve either objective.

✓ **For the founder or owner of the company**: Saying you want to go public, yet all you really want is to sell your company and get out, will stress your company as it tries to achieve both goals.

✓ **For the seasoned executive**: Saying you want to change the world, but you really just want to have control over your future, are two fundamentally different desires yielding inconsistent results.

Yes, multiple objectives can coexist. But to ensure success it is critical to align your fundamental desires with your goals for your company.

What are your limitations?

There are many two, ten and even twenty-five year old start-ups, in which the CEO is the reason for the company's success *and* the reason the company has not met everyone's growth expectations. I call this the "Rubber Band Theory," which is illustrated below. Initially, if you plot the entrepreneur's or CEO's abilities (as measured by management and leadership capability, openness to learn and improve, etc.) over that of a fast-growth company's performance (as measured by revenue, profits, market share, etc.), the leader *is the reason* the company thrives. The drive and stewardship exhibited by the founder lifts the company's performance and causes growth. That is, the leader *pulls up* company performance. But as the company adds more people, and competition becomes more complex, and the market more sophisticated, the company gradually becomes more difficult to manage. If the leader's capabilities do not outpace that of the company's, then the leader *pulls down* company performance.

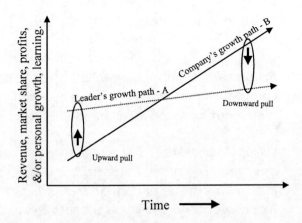

Leaders have limitations. The more defensive you are in challenging your own limitations, the more difficult it is for you to learn, adapt, and continue to be of immense value to your company.

✓ **Personal:** The ability to create, build, and then lead your company to new heights requires an ability to set aside your personal hang-ups and move forward. In this way, you make the slope of your personal curve "A" steeper than the company's curve "B" and can maintain upward momentum. Two personality traits investors watch for in company leaders that can cause them to avoid investing in the business are:

Need to control: One way that leaders pull down their company is to insist on being in the approval cycle for every decision, no matter how large or small, no matter what area, and no matter who is in charge of that area.

Need to maintain majority ownership: Entrepreneurs tend to have the notion that they can own a majority of their company throughout its life cycle. Although this can be true, when you need outside capital, it is totally reasonable for investors to require ownership interest. If money is so easy to come by and ideas are so valuable, why isn't everyone looking for ideas instead of money?

✓ **Professional:** Your personal style is reflected in your company's performance. When assessing your influence, watch out for these areas:

Where do you stand relative to the organizational maturity of your company? Too often, a company led by the founder is built around his or her particular area of expertise. Are you too techie or too salesy? Do you believe project management is too bureaucratic? Is your organization unbalanced?

How do you respond to your company's internal systems? Do you abhor process or internal information systems, because you feel they are the antithesis of results?

Planning maturity: Do you have a cohesive strategy and flexible business plan, or an unchanging plan? Do you find project planning is a waste of time? Leaders who plan for risk are able to accept even more risk.

Business maturity: How are you at cash management? Are you able to prioritize? Can you make the tough decisions that are required to grow in a controlled manner, including *not* trying to do everything or enter every market at once?

Leadership: Do you have, and can you articulate, a clear vision? Are you autocratic, or too laissez-faire? These attributes will be reflected in your company.

✓ **Financial:** The biggest question for the start-up entrepreneur is, "Are you ready to go bankrupt?" How much money in reserve do you have? Most entrepreneurs I meet feel their idea is so great that all it will take is a few months and they will have all the investment capital they need. This is rarely the case. Especially in today's environment. Since investors generally bet on the jockey and not the horse, your idea had better come with a great management team, unique value proposition, sustainable competitive advantage, and huge market potential. After all, if you are not willing to put your life savings into your idea, why should an investor?

How do you overcome your limits?

There are several ways to overcome the challenges of leading your company to new heights. The first is to recognize that improvement requires change. There is an old saying, "The definition of insanity is doing the same things while expecting significantly different results." So what different things can you do?

✓ **Accept limitations:** One way to win is to embrace who you are, make the required decisions to put your company first, and then do what *you* do best. This might mean being the best sales person the company has, or running new technology development. Apply whatever strengths you have in order for the company to win.

✓ **Significantly change:** Take some notes on what you have learned each year over the last ten years. You will find that it takes a very long time to learn life lessons. If your company can wait for you to learn these lessons, great. However, the time it takes for you to significantly change might not match the short time your company requires to survive and thrive.

✓ **Seek help:** One sure way to bring in new ideas is to get outside assistance. Which is why it is so important to have an outside board of advisors or board of directors. If chosen wisely, the people on the board can help you through the tumultuous maze of building a business, and provide you with reality checks for your company and sanity checks for you. Lawyers, accountants, consultants and bankers can also be a great source of advice and counsel. By trying to go it alone, your road is surely tougher and the chances for success are certainly not as high as they could be otherwise.

What are you getting into?

There is no way to know what cards you will be dealt. However, you can stack the deck in your favor by knowing what you want, understanding your limitations, and resolving to do something about them. Then make the difficult decisions as early as possible. A careful assessment of yourself and your company's situation, and purposeful course setting, is essential if your company is to reach its next level.

What are the Core Values Of Leading CEOs?

Ever wonder what other CEOs' core values are? What company leaders rank as their highest priorities in leading their company? Or what they value most? This chapter looks at what CEOs desire from their companies and provides insights into their thinking.

A survey through an American Electronics Association (now, TechAmerica) task force was conducted with 22 CEOs from software and electronics companies in Oregon's "Silicon Forest." They were asked to describe their core business values and share the mental picture that came to mind when imagining their ideal company. The responses were grouped into categories, and the percentages show how many CEOs had specific comments about that particular category. Compare and contrast your own values against those of these CEOs to gain a better understanding of how to take your company to its next level. The answers can be very enlightening.

Question 1: What are Your Core Business Values?

✓ **Employee Satisfaction (77%)** Within this major category, four major areas were identified: satisfied employees, empowerment, employee development, and pro-active employees. The leaders who mentioned these values stated as follows:

  • *Satisfied employees* (100%) Leaders know that people are key to corporate performance. They strive to ensure their employees' views are heard, that they share in rewards and celebrate victories, and they believe that employees should work in a positive, even fun atmosphere. Maintaining a professional environment and ensuring job satisfaction are very important, as is respect for every employees' worth. One CEO stated "Provide a professional environment which challenges creativity and rewards accomplishments."

- *Empowered employees* (58%) It is important for leaders to empower their employees, encourage autonomy and decision making at the lowest levels, allow employees to speak their minds, and have open and honest communications.

- *Pro-active employees* (42%) Leaders look for people who take initiative and calculated risks and encourage them to challenge the system. They seek those who take responsibility, and create opportunities for employees to step up to difficult situations.

- *Employee development* (32%) CEOs also feel that change is constant in business and this requires people who can and will adapt and improve. And they support their employees through these development and growth transitions.

✓ **Customer Satisfaction (77%)** Leaders also found it essential to understand and satisfy customers' needs. "Our success is dependent upon defining and providing solutions to our customers' requirements," one CEO stated.

- *Meet or exceed needs and expectations* (100%) Responsiveness to customers, satisfying their needs, and maintaining a high level of customer satisfaction is very important. Being easy to do business with and providing impeccable customer service is also essential.

- *Customer focus* (45%) An adjunct to this is having an intense customer focus, seeing them as partners, and striving for their happiness with products and services.

- *Understand needs and expectations* (36%) Knowing and meeting commitments to their customers is an essential part of many leaders' core business values.

✓ **Process (68%)** The ability to define the operational process by which customers' needs are identified and met is a significant component of the CEOs' values. The results of doing so enable them to repeatedly exceed expectations and provide high quality service. Defining operational processes also makes it possible to continually improve efficiency and effectiveness, which ultimately increases competitiveness and profitability. As one CEO said, "Our standard is products and services which satisfy the requirements of our customers with consistent, dependable, and predictable performance."

✓ **Leadership & Management (59%)** Permeating all core values is the need to lead teams to repeatable greatness by honest, open example. "Consistent and stable leadership… values are a foundation for developing our strategic plan," said one CEO.

- *Honesty & Integrity* (100%) Those running companies expect high integrity, professionalism, and ethical behavior from themselves and their employees. They want to win honestly and they want to show fairness in all their business dealings.

- *Leadership* (64%) Consistency and communication are common elements of leadership, so that employees and the management team understand and buy into the company's values, vision and mission.

- *Teamwork* (50%) CEOs feel that winning together, with a common attitude of involvement, is important to success.

- *Communicate management performance* (50%) It is also important to share how the company is doing in an open manner. This includes knowing what information is suitable to tell employees, and how to use it for continuous improvement.

✓ **Shareholder Satisfaction (55%)** Those individuals who invest in the company are on the minds of company leaders. "Protect and increase the value of shareholders' investment," is a common comment.

- *Profitability* (100%) Leaders are in business to make a profit. They wish to provide a superior product and receive superior revenue for it.
- *Growth* (38%) They seek to aggressively improve market share and grow the company.
- *Asset appreciation* (38%) And they insist on protecting and increasing the value of their shareholders' investments.

✓ **Community (23%)** In addition to all the business-related core values, leaders want to improve the community by being good corporate citizens. They want to "Contribute to the quality of life in the communities, in which we work and live."

✓ **Product / technology (23%)** For high-technology companies, CEOs "Strive to be recognized as a technology leader in products and services."

✓ **Market Leadership (18%)** Being the first with the best, by being market experts, is a critical part of leaders' business values. "Market leadership of a significant growing market segment is mandatory."

✓ **Supplier Partnership (18%)** Last, but not least, these executives want to "Treat suppliers as if they are our best customers."

Question 2: What is the ideal company?

In addition to the question of core values, each CEO was asked what image came to mind when thinking of their ideal company. The answers fell into the same major categories as the core values, except the number of CEOs specifying each category shifted.

- ✓ Leadership & Management – 77%
- ✓ Employee satisfaction – 68%
- ✓ Shareholder satisfaction – 36%
- ✓ Process – 32%
- ✓ Customer satisfaction – 27%
- ✓ Community – 18%
- ✓ Market leadership – 18%
- ✓ Product / technology – 14%

These results indicate that the ideal company has exceptional leadership, which will help address all the other core business values. In fact, these results point to the importance of solid leadership and a management team, which leads to employee satisfaction and a company poised to accomplish significant corporate objectives.

Do your core values match?

In searching to identify and communicate your own core values, take time to determine what is really important to you and the company's stakeholders, including employees, customers, shareholders, vendors, and the community. Assess your company's strengths relative to its processes, products, technology and management. Are there common goals throughout the company? Are these goals driven by a desire to grow the company, make a profit and improve the community, through exceptional team-oriented problem solving?

In developing and communicating your core business values, assess your priorities relative to your fellow CEOs' priorities and lead your company to accomplish your highest expectations.

A Simple Secret to Successful Leadership

There is a very simple, yet very effective, secret to successfully running companies. Actually, it is based on an equation that is easy to learn and straightforward to use. This formula can help you guide an entire company, whether only 5 or 5,000 employees. Obviously there are many secrets to success, but this one is particularly effective, in that it can be applied to many situations. It can also help greatly focus an organization.

Secret to Success: What is this equation? It is simply:

$$S = G \times P \times A \times M^{sm}$$

In this case, "S" represents Success, "G" is Goals, "P" means Planning, "A" stands for Action, and "M" is short for Motivation. Notice that these elements are multiplicative: If any one of these critical factors is zero, success is zero. They all need to be well represented and balanced to maximize success for you, your customers, your company and stockholders.

Success: Although there are varying degrees of success, high-quality organizations try to outperform their competition by a *large* margin. So do winning entrepreneurs, and so do excellent employees.

Success defines the finish line... "When do we know we are done?"

Goals: In order to succeed, you need a clearly defined vision for your company. What are your corporate objectives? Personal objectives? What are you shooting for? Whether it is financial gain, market share, personal improvement, or socially driven principles, having clear objectives is the first place to start – on the path to success. Goals should be "SMART": Specific, Measurable, Attainable, Realistic and Time-constrained. Otherwise, they are not goals, they are desires, or worse, merely ideas.

Goals define the "what"… "What are we striving for?"

Planning: According to some management "gurus", organizations should not plan, they should "just do it". Hogwash. It is essential to take enough time to plan. Write down stated goals. Specify how you are going to achieve your goals, then communicate them, obtain feedback and consensus from those tasked with the efforts, and modify the goals and objectives accordingly. This exercise actually creates a buy-in process. It is skipped so often that disaster sometimes overcomes the greatest intentions. The value of planning as an organizational communication tool cannot be overstressed. In fact, only when plans are written, communicated and argued over will the optimal path be defined and real long-term lessons become learnable. The next iteration involves dusting off the prior plan and changing what did not work. Outperforming your competitors - and yourself - in the long run requires that companies include lessons-learned as part of their core values.

Planning defines the "how"… "How do we get there from here?"

Actions: This is where implementation determines the outcome. Imagine the success a well-run organization can have, with agreed-upon targets (goals), a map of how to get there, and required resources (plan), and a clear picture of the responsibilities of every department and employee?

Actions define the "who"… "Who is going to implement the plan?"

Motivation: An underlying factor in the entire equation is how people feel about the direction of the company. "What's in it for me," both personally and organizationally, determines how well individual motives line up with the corporate direction. Without some level of motivation, the whole thing can fall apart.

Motivation defines the "why"... "Why are we doing this project?"

Throughout these four major elements, there are certainly others: For example, accountability – ensuring a system is in place for assigning and measuring people's actions and contributions to the plan; and leadership – which makes the make-or-break difference in successfully implementing this equation.

The secret to using this equation is that each factor needs to be considered. Use this equation to guide your attention *equally* to setting goals, planning, implementing your plan, and motivating your team. If any one of these factors is ignored to the point that it approaches zero, so does your possbility for success.

Change Leadership: Taking Your company to New Heights

CEOs are driven to achieve great personal and corporate performance. They want to succeed. They want to exceed customers' expectations and they want to trounce the competition. To accomplish this, CEOs regularly define and work towards difficult goals. To overcome the great obstacles this entails usually requires significant change within the company. Examples of change are: Product development methods. Financial systems. Organizational structure. Operational workflow. Marketing & Sales processes.

Many change programs end in failure not because new technologies or processes were brought into the company, but *how* management attempted to integrate changes within the company. The change process can be very difficult and should be addressed in a way that improves *buy-in by those who are affected* and increases the probability of success: for individuals, for teams and for the company.

Positive cycle of change: In order to affect positive change, there are specific 'steps' CEOs and change leaders need to take. In fact, these steps are required to ensure buy-in and support by affected organizations and *reinforce openness to change.*

✓ **Inform and involve:** The first step is to create an environment of openness and trust. This can best be accomplished by informing and involving those who are affected by the change. Leaders can best set up for positive change by acknowledging change is difficult and remaining flexible to the outcome. In this way, your employees recognize you understand how tough change can be. Communicating why change is required and sharing corporate objectives and risks of not changing helps employees understand why you're undertaking the process. Involving them with the change process dramatically increases buy-in, in that they start taking ownership of the change – which can yield profound and lasting results. Lacking this step supports suspicion and ultimately failure of successful change.

✓ **Explore personal opportunities and value:** Through the 'involve and inform' step, everyone can explore what the change means to them as well as the company. This occurs naturally, so why not accept this as part of the change process? This is a great way to align personal goals with company goals and should fit in with the strategic, business and operational planning that you already do. If employees and managers extract value out of the change, so should the company.

✓ **Building a participatory change effort:** Exploring personal opportunities stimulates creativity in solving significant problems, overcoming tough challenges and implementing difficult change. And it helps organizations rise to the challenges being faced with pride of ownership that an open and trusting company evokes. Soliciting continuous feedback helps the change process move forward. The results of corporate change are only as good as the acceptance of each individual who is affected by it – so constant communication is essential.

Negative cycle of change: There are some sure-fire ways to doom change to failure. *These three major steps reinforce resistance to change:*

✓ **Unknown / uninformed / uninvolved:** A 'golden rule' of change is "get those who are affected by change to participate in the change." If people are neither informed nor involved in the process, they will resist change.

✓ **Personal fear of change:** They will also be threatened by change and because they won't know what's going on, they will fear the 'unknown' of change. People commonly go through a cycle of "It's new, therefore I fear it, therefore, it's bad."

✓ **Individual defensiveness:** When someone thinks they have no control over their environment, nor what happens to their job, organization or future, they can become defensive and either avoid or 'attack' the change – overtly or worse, covertly.

One approach to consider: The Malcolm Baldridge Award looks at improvement by testing [1] the concept, [2] deployment, and [3] results. If the *concept* for change is not sound, then obviously, it should be abandoned. Change plans require thoughtful and open discussions to work out implementation problems before they appear. Doing so in a team environment helps initiate the buy-in process. Once the concept is worked through, if it cannot be *deployed* throughout the affected organizations, it's as good as no change at all – or worse, a negative change. Once the change is successfully deployed, the *results* need to be measured to see if the original objectives are being met. If not, make adjustments and re-measure.

Involve, inform and communicate: Instant global access through e-mail can sometimes be mistaken for communication. (Witness Radio Shack's email firing.) Personal, team or company conversations about personal desires, team goals, or corporate objectives can spark creative solutions to difficult problems, encourage joint risk-taking and can dramatically improve corporate performance. Dealing with the fear of the unknown, giving feedback on progress and listening as change efforts proceed are tools the CEO can use to take her / his company to its next level of performance.

Your Leadership Style: Inspiring Followership

At the *beginning* of the day, the CEO either leads a team to accomplish very difficult objectives & meet business objectives… or not. Everyone knows when the company has exceeded expectations. And they know when this has not happened. With everything that's happening in the world today, CEOs can have a tough time keeping employees focused - and need to ask themselves: How do I *inspire* people to follow me? How can employees be led - to focus most of their efforts towards achieving a company's never-changing desire for growth and improvement, in an ever-changing world?

The answers boil down to two major areas. [1] Find out what your managers and employees want and them help them achieve it, and [2] Lead by example. When I have failed to understand employees' motivations, I have failed to lead. In one instance, when I put in the 14 to 16 hour days required to lead a company, within a few weeks the normal workday of 9:30am to 3:00pm shifted to 7:00am to 6:00pm, and amazing things happened – including having even *more* fun. Long workdays don't always translate to more fun, but on tough projects or short deadlines, having employees wake up excited to come to work, make a difference, and accomplish significant goals – because their leader is there, with them - can transform an organization.

So, what should we do to encourage our employees to follow us?

✓ **Communicate company goals, objectives and performance**. By sharing your mission and how the company is doing, employees will buy into your increasing demands, and be better able to handle more knowledgeable customers and tougher competitors. Clear communication can couple company strategies with employee efforts. Developing a "strategies to tactics" approach unites employees and increases performance. Balancing effectiveness with efficiencies ensures resources are focused on repeatable results. Increasing communication throughout the organization provides feedback on the mission, strategies and objectives; and ensures they are in line with employees' abilities (and resources) to carry out their necessary efforts.

✓ **Instill a sense of ownership and entrepreneurialism,** on a person-by-person and project-by-project basis. This leadership must be by example. Encouraging risk allows every person to step up to the increasing challenges of a complex world. Ownership of projects and products, and continuous process improvement, reduces turn-over. Matching responsibility with accountability, from the most senior executive to the lowest level employee, encourages employees to raise their level of performance. Balancing short-term results with a focus on the future creates constancy of purpose. Aligning core values and organizational vision with customers' needs focuses everyone on the real mission.

✓ **Ensure every employee is working to satisfy customers' needs**. An intense customer focus moves the organization towards value-adding efforts. An intense customer focus is obvious to every customer and helps your company become recognized as the preferred partner / solution provider.

✓ **Instill loyalty and trust** by viewing employees as the resources they are, instead of only seeing them as the costs they incur. So often, troubles with excess inventory or accounts receivable are blamed on employees instead of management… who typically are the ones responsible for the decisions in the first place. Empowered people who trust your leadership will solve very difficult problems. The days of a command and control system where all knowledge comes from the top are over. Valuing "local knowledge" as an asset to be maximized results in effectively-made, smarter decisions. Again, loyalty and trust improves the bottom line. Managing by fact, instead of politics, increases information's impact on decisions.

✓ **Involve and inform employees in critical company changes**. This increases their acceptance of change and leads to improvements in the changes themselves. It also increases your employees' value by using *their* ideas to support company objectives, which increases employee buy-in immeasurably.

✓ **Synergize your organization, management system and resources**. Balance *who* (organization) does the work, with *how* (process) it gets done, and ensure employees are trained so they have the *ability* to increase performance. This will bolster their sense that you really do care about your employees, and will earn their long-term trust.

✓ **Build an environment of open interdepartmental communication**. Developing cross-functional, team-oriented employees is more difficult than it sounds. Effectively implementing this approach supports conflict resolution instead of conflict avoidance, and also breaks down internal barriers. Developing an environment of mutual respect and trust leads to creative and calculated risk-taking, and is essential to succeed with global competition. A predictive instead of a reactive operating mode provides a return on time invested by an order of magnitude. This, in turn, reduces crises management. Fun and fortune can be the result.

✓ **Encourage continuous personal development**. Implementing appropriate new tools and techniques can result in a huge increase in employee productivity. Just as the right tools can dramatically reduce time spent fixing a car's engine, so can the right organizational tools enhance performance. Continual organizational learning should be part of management's internal processes. Again, outside help and support in training can provide valuable return on investment.

Management is about process, projects, organizations, creating and implementing marketing and business plans, and all the other elements that go into making sure a company runs as efficiently and as effectively as possible. However, *leadership* is all about people. It is about having your employees follow you through an arduous journey to accomplish incredible objectives, while making sure everyone feels great about it. This is especially true in tough economic or uncertain times.

As you recall your fondest moments in a company - the most exhilarating experiences can occur when a disparate team pulls together to tackle an urgent and possibly corporate-life threatening situation. With the concerted effort of a well coordinated team, and the vision and leadership of a true leader, projects are completed ahead of schedule, or the new plant is up and operating in time, or the competition is blown away by a new product.

In other words, the mission is accomplished. And through inspiring "followership," your missions can be bolder and your results even greater.

How to Bankrupt Your Company Without Really Trying

As I write this chapter, it occurs to me that over the past couple decades of consulting and interim executive work; I have seen the same problems and mistakes over and over again. When you are in the middle of day-to-day crises, personnel problems, customers' demands, and market shifts, the reasons for "why things go wrong" can elude the best of us.

My thoughts are written so that you might rise above *your* operational melee and see if these apply to you in any small way. The items on these lists should ring alarm bells to you and your management team. This list is valid if you are just starting a company or trying to take your company to its next level.

1. <u>Assuming only start-up costs for your business plan's financials</u>: All too often, entrepreneurs just list the costs they think they will incur to start the company. "What other costs could there be?" some have asked me. Without an understanding of *cash flow* (plus an income statement & balance sheet to support the cash flow), you can't perform "what-if" assessments. What if the sales cycle is longer than expected? What if accounts receivable take 60 days instead of 35 days? What if we hire those three people two months later instead of immediately? No one ever went out of business because they had too much money. Projecting your cash needs is essential to successfully charting your course. Without it, you're flying blind.

2. <u>Too detailed</u>: Entrepreneurs tend to think that if they could just convey all the great information they've amassed, investors will simply have to write a check. I've actually seen a 117-page business plan. Unbelievable. Who has time to wade through that plan? And how can employees implement it?

3. <u>Too vague / too general</u>: On the other side of the coin, just stating that "According to 'so & so,' " the market will be $1.3 trillion by the year 2020." is too broad a statement, which doesn't explain how you'll sell just *one* customer. This caught the imagination of the investment community in the Dot.Bomb era, but not any more.

4. <u>Risks not identified</u>: It is easy to be enamoured by the upside and excited to become a leader in some new market area. But it can also make for a rude awakening when you haven't taken the time to account nor plan for an "I gotcha" that puts you out of business. Identifying risks can actually be an optimist's method for making darn sure that there is cash available in the operational budget to deal with problems that will arise.

5. <u>Assuming the sales cycle is 0</u>: I've lost count of how many times financial statements will show a sales person hired in July with sales increasing that month. What is the learning curve for each sales person? How long will it take for them to be 100% efficient? Sometimes up to six months are required before they're hitting on all eight cylinders.

6. <u>No assumptions in financials</u>: Every financial statement has a set of assumptions, whether you state them explicitly or not. Might as well state them. Some examples of fundamental assumptions that should be understood for every financial statement are shown at the end of this chapter.

7. "We have no competition:" This is the most-used red flag there is. If what you have developed is, in fact, brand new, the single largest impediment to adoption of your product / service is that people have to change to use it. It can take a whole generation for people to change behavior. And a decision to not purchase it is the same as competition. Underestimate this at your own risk.

8. Any "social media" positioning: Ugh. There's serious money to be made by applying Web 3.0 (or 4.0, or…) technology to a business. (It can be done. I ran a company and led the effort to create and sell a web-based information service, which generated a net operating profit of over 80% within a month after it's launch, in 1996.) Just make sure your "web company" is enabling someone else to make money in some sort of traditional way (if B2B). In fact, if technology is seen as the tool it is, instead of a business model it is not, you will be better in the long run.

9. Not sure who your customers are: I've seen many companies not *really* know who their customers are, why they're buying, nor how they buy. Without this knowledge (gained through customer / prospect research), you're just shooting moving targets in the dark. These days, there's not enough ammunition (capital) around to do this. This is explored in more detail, later.

10. "We're going to capture X% of the market:" A corollary to the "too vague" red flag is that the CEO / management team build their expectations around capturing 5 or 10 or 25 percent of the market. The real acid test is how you're going to sell your product to just *one* customer, and then how cost-effectively you can replicate this sale.

11. "I am the management team:" Very often, the CEO feels s/he can do everything and is afraid to give up control of the company. If you want to seriously grow, get over it. Your company is best

served by your ability to make outstanding strategic decisions, not in the day to day operations that tend to bog you down. If you hire the best, they will pay for themselves many times over. Being closed to other opinions is a sure way to bankrupt your company.

12. <u>Too focused on the product</u>: Very often (especially in technology-based companies), the founder and/or management team is enamoured with the product – which comes across in day to day decisions. This can lead to the inability to morph the product to meet an even larger market demand. In charting your company's course (through a business plan), the product / service is but one part of the entire 'story' to be told. Typically, not enough time or efforts are spent on the opportunity or need.

13. <u>"We're going to 'focus' on five different markets</u>:" I've seen this in start-ups and Fortune 500 companies alike. If you have one dollar and need to spend it on one market, which one will you choose? Why? (Answer: Highest ROI.) Then why would you spend money on any other market? Sometimes a second market requires the company be organized differently. This can be the fastest way to ruin your company.

14. <u>No outside Board of Directors / Advisors</u>: An "outside" team can be your savior. With additional people looking out for your best interests, you'll have access to an unbelievable talent pool. People who have "been there and done that" can save you significant time, money, and maybe even your company. Select them wisely, pay them well, and respect their time.

15. <u>"Market share matters more than revenue" / "Revenue matters more than profits" / "Profits matter more than cash flow</u>:" Careful – Customers may be King, but Cash is Queen. Meaning – you have to keep them both happy. Focusing on market share causes decisions to be made that typically includes lowering price instead of delivering value. And delivering value

is essential to being able to argue why your offering is the best around (if it is).

16. Viral marketing: Sounds great. Doesn't work as well as everyone assumes. If this is how your customers make buying decisions, great. (Having performed customer research for many companies, "web" has only been as high as #3, on the list of how people make a purchase-decision. Never the #1 method.)

17. The technology will sell itself: Sounds great. Doesn't work.

18. "Just do it:" The shoot-from-the-hip approach is fine if you have tons of experience and lots of cash on your side, but few companies can afford this luxury. Yet most companies act as if they are immune to the effects of decisions made on insufficient information, or "idea-of-the-quarter" with little or no planning. Remember the equation "S=G x P x A x M" (Success equals Goals times Planning times Action times Motivation). If there is no real planning, success is much more difficult to achieve.

It is very difficult to get all of these things right, especially at the same time. But in many cases, if one of these issues goes unresolved for a few months, you may quickly find your company in a downward revenue spiral. And that could be disastrous.

Sidebar: Business Assumptions

Some examples - of fundamental assumptions that should be understood for every financial projection:

- Accounts Receivable
- Anticipated Bad Debt
- Available Credit Line
- Benefits & Taxes
- Business Insurance
- Capital Equipment Lease Term
- Combined Federal & State Tax Rate
- Depreciation
- Headcount (per department)
- Interest Expense On Capital Equipment Lease, Credit Line, & On Long Term Borrowings
- Inventory (if applicable)
- Long Term Borrowings Term
- Maximum Credit Line Used
- Minimum Office Space
- Office Rent
- Lease / Maintenance Expense
- Salary Increases
- Sales Commissions
- Sales Cycle
- Term of Office Lease
- Total Sales Through Commissions
- Utilities Expense

How to Develop Your Strategic Plan in Two Days.

Everyone tells you how important strategic planning is. But how can you spend time on this 'year-long' process when you have to respond to every customers' wishes, your boards' needs, your banker's request for last quarter's financials, and just making payroll? Your day-to-day challenges make it tough, if not impossible, to do any long-term thinking, let alone planning.

Now, in just two short days at an 'off-site' you can assess the competitive situation, your company's critical success factors, align your management team and develop sufficient planning to plot the future of your company in ways you never thought possible.

Here's how to do it:
Follow the steps identified below, and for each section use the *Affinity Diagramming* process to brainstorm each issue. This will generate 30 to 80 prioritized and organized ideas (instead of the usual 3 to 5), that can then be used to build your company's case for strategic shifts to ultimately maximize revenue:

(1) **Define the over-riding purpose of the strategic planning session**: Typically it's to gain consensus on your company's strategic priorities and on probable ways to address them. It is to identify you-bet-your-company issues, and come to consensus about how to deal with them. In a team-oriented way.

(2) **Define the rules for the group session:** It will be difficult to garner everyone's thoughts easily. You'll need to help each other get through the process smoothly. A facilitator – skilled in strategic planning – can be of immense help in successfully guiding you through the process to efficiently gain insights you need to make effective strategic decisions.

(3) **Situation Analysis**: Get consensus on the key (helping and hurting) external environmental trends that may have significant impact on the company's future performance. These include:

- **Internal / External Assessment**: Determine major areas of strengths to leverage, weaknesses to bolster, opportunities to take advantage of, and threats to neutralize.

- **General Environment**: Determine major technology, economy, society, regulatory, and political trends that can - and most likely will - affect your company in both the short & long term.

- **Industry Environment**: Clearly articulate your markets, their needs, industry trends, competition in defined markets, barriers to entry, assumptions you've made in the past and need to make in the future, and substitute products / services.

- **Customers Needs**: Do you really know (specifically) who they are, what they buy, why they buy, and how they buy? Without any guesswork? Are your internal organization and systems supporting your success?

- **Summary of Strategic issues**: Come to a consensus as to what the most critical top-level strategic issues are.

(4) **Financial Assessment**: Define and communicate what the "no change" expectations are and then define and compare against the *expected* growth. Agree on the baseline financial forecast,, the results expected in the future if no strategic or structural

changes are made in the business, and – at a very high level – agree on the desired future financial picture. Identify any critical financial issues that need to be addressed (i.e. - cash flow, profitability, spending, funding). Present past three years financial history and three-year forecast, amount of cash needed for investment and understand the critical difference between goals and commitments. (This takes more CEO's guidance than the rest – as s/he provides the vision for the company.)

(5) **Strategic Alternatives**: Identify the top most-probable strategic alternatives / initiatives, their pluses and minuses given the company's strengths & weaknesses, probable financial and market situation / forecasts and the steps that must be taken to evaluate them, and decide which to pursue. Recognize these alternatives will drive cash and profit requirements. What are the risks and probable financial outcomes of each alternative? You'll need to choose the right alternatives before the market chooses for you.

(6) **Strategic Priority Issues**: Identify the top strategic priority issues that must be addressed by the company. These are typically those that:

- Have a long term and positive financial impact
- Address a fleeting market window
- Are critical to any 'stop the bleeding' issues

These come from the SWOT assessment, and generally meet one or more of these criteria:

- Deals with identified trends
- Addresses a changing window of opportunity
- Are critical to fix or correct any key structural weaknesses
- Things you can do internally to affect change

(7) **Key Results Areas / Critical Success Factors**: Define the areas and metrics that the organization will use to establish objectives and to measure strategic and financial success. This is typically an area of business activity in which the

business must excel to meet customer needs, beat competition, and meet stakeholders' expectations.

(8) **Specific 3 to 5 year objectives**: Based on the strategic alternatives & direction defined earlier in the session, determine the core three to five objectives which should be met over the next three to five years. Examples are: market share, geographic presence, services offered, etc.

(9) **Specific 6 months to 1 year goals**: Based on the three to five year objectives developed above, determine the core three to five objectives which should be met over the next six to twelve months. (Close ratios, costs to acquire customers, etc.)

Using this process, you can use your understanding of the world around you to plot a course for the next three to five years, and more importantly, gain insights into what you **need** to do in the coming months to effectively do what's required to meet those long term objectives. You can then determine the costs associated with the plans you've developed, and iterate the planning as required until you develop an operational game plan that is affordable, achievable and effective in helping your company achieve the results you know your company can achieve. Will it be done in two days? Strategic planning is *never* done. But you can codify your critical efforts to be accomplished and plot out the best course possible from where you are today.

If it sounds easy, it's not. In fact, pre-work is required in order for the session to go smoothly and provide valuable information upon which to build and implement you-bet-your-company strategies. Effective follow-up is also essential to actually implementing changes needed to dramatically improve your results... and *results* are ultimately what business is all about.

Section 2

Building Your Company

- **How to Build Your Company**
- **Raising Money in a Tight Market**
- **Building Your Game Plan**
- **Building Your Team**
- **Building Your Story**
- **Creating Your Stock Structure**
- **Building Credibility**
- **The Realities of Raising Money**

The purpose of this section is to address those elements in creating a company that are neglected or misunderstood by many entrepreneurs seeking to get their company to their next levels. Starting a company so that investors are compelled to invest requires the same decisions as trying to bootstrap the company to be profitable. Today's economic environment requires a professional perspective. This section is intended to lend a helping hand to those entrepreneurs who seriously want to build a successful and growth-oriented company.

How to Build Your Company

Of the hundreds of entrepreneurs I know, have met &/or helped, most have had a great idea and want to build a business around that idea. They are passionate and typically won't take "No." for an answer. This is a good thing. And potentially bad – relative to building your company.

From Square One
Questions I've been asked include: What is the best way to build a company? What should I do first? I have limited resources, so how do I move this idea forward, in the most cost-effective way possible?

Although there is no one right answer, there are actions you can take to get your company started on the right foot. Looking at the diagram below, consider the following notions, which we will address further, in this chapter:

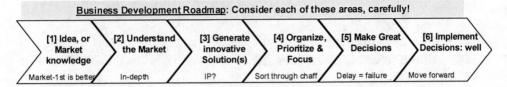

Business Development Roadmap: Consider each of these areas, carefully!

[1] Idea, or Market knowledge	[2] Understand the Market	[3] Generate innovative Solution(s)	[4] Organize, Prioritize & Focus	[5] Make Great Decisions	[6] Implement Decisions: well
Market-1st is better	In-depth	IP?	Sort through chaff	Delay = failure	Move forward

[1&2] If there is no market, the best idea in the world will not launch a company. Is your idea viable?

[3] If you have trouble generating innovative solutions for a known market need, it will be difficult to differentiate yourself form others.

[4] If it is difficult for you to organize all the disparate information coming at you, sort through all the noise in the marketplace and prioritize so that you know what comes first, second, etc., or you will languish in analysis paralysis.

[5] If you have a hard time making decisions, the market may pass you by. Or competitors will seize the opportunity you have identified.

[6] If implementation is not your strong suit, then all your hard work will be for naught.

How do you work through these areas? (Or overcome these obstacles, if any of these areas is a problem?) If you have the years it takes to learn, great. If not... bring together the talent to "make it so".

Idea or Market Knowledge

Most entrepreneurs develop a business because they have a great idea. Sometimes, entrepreneurs have market experience. In either case, the first thing on the To-Do list is usually "Go raise money". Clearly, if you have a great idea, all you need is money, because that's all it really takes. Right? Wrong.

Satchel Paige's statement *"None of us is as smart as all of us"* is highly applicable in this situation. This implies that you'll need to build a team. Maybe even hire your own boss (a CEO). More importantly, *none of us is as smart as the market.*

If you have never built a successful business, chances are you don't *really* know what it takes to cost-effectively build a successful company. You may think you do, but after helping many entrepreneurs get to their next level(s), I am surprised by how many (later) admit to not having a clue about what it *really* took to build their company. Chances are you don't, either. I certainly had no clue what building my own company would entail, 18 years ago.

Even though I was previously in the top 2% of – and had led 250 people in line and project roles in – a Global 500 company. Being an executive in business does not equal being an entrepreneur in a start-up. Even if you have market knowledge, assuming that you know what customers think or will think can be disastrous to your company. This is why investors want to know about the market. First.

Understand the Market
There is so much to cover on this topic, just (what I think are) the two most-important aspects are addressed:

✓ Is there a "there", there? The best way to answer this question is to find out what people will *pay* for your product or service. If it's more than you think you should charge, you're leaving money on the table. If it's less, then you should reconsider your solution, or reconsider if you should even build this company. It's not only the best knowledge you can gain at this point, it is unethical to ask for investment capital without knowing the true value for yourself. "What will you pay for it?" is the wrong question. Elsewhere in The Entrepreneur's Survival Guide, a way is outlined for you to determine the market's true assessment of your solution's value.

✓ How do you cost-effectively reach your best customers? There is a way to answer some sub-tier questions, like: Who are your best customers (who pay the most, the soonest, and refer others to you), What do they really want? Why do they want it? How do you reach them – in the most cost-effective way(s) possible. With this information, you will be able to sketch out your plan. Without it, you will just be assuming, which = guessing. The answers to these four questions (which need to be assessed, statistically, written down, and shared with others you trust to provide valuable feedback) will yield your best Market, Message, and Method. Without this information, you will be *unable* to write a business plan. Or at least not one that will easily get funded.

You may find that you need to go back to your original idea and make some changes.

Generate Innovative Solutions

Only after you truly understand market nuances should you develop a solution that addresses it. If you speed to the development stage without understanding *who* will place *what* value on it, you will probably just be spinning your wheels.

This requires creativity and the ability to ensure that your creativity is focused on real, implementable and marketable solutions. That is, you may need to iterate a few times to zero in on the most valuable, least-cost solutions to market needs.

Once you've validated your solution in the marketplace (through market research, not yet developing a product.), you will be well on your way to being *able* to plan your business in more detail, and do away with assumptions you may have.

If you don't have the inherent skills or experience to do this, then find others who do. The process of "selling" them on your business is an essential skill in building your company.

Organize, Prioritize & Focus

If you are innovative, or have started building an innovative team, this is the part where you'll need to ensure that all the "great" ideas are vetted – relative to the business needs. That is, just because you have one or a hundred great ideas, you'll need to sort through all of these and determine which ones yield the greatest ability to move your company forward. Not hold it back, because you are trying to create too much in that first product release. Out of 100 ideas, there is undoubtedly a

"Pareto chart" you could apply as to the Return on Investment (ROI), and therefore value to your fledgling company.

If you don't have the ability to quickly sort through the multiple solutions you *could* develop, find someone who can. By the way… this type of person is worth their weight in gold: Quickly and correctly sorting through all the options to focus on what will be the home run is not a trait everyone has. Although many think they do. Proven experience, in the form of a "hired-gun CEO", may be required to turbo-charge your company forward. Don't underestimate this person.

Make Great Decisions
The only control an entrepreneur has is over his/her ability to make decisions. Poor decisions get poor results, while great decisions (may) get great results. I say "may", because making great decisions is mandatory, but not sufficient – in order to start and successfully build your company.

Taking too long to make decisions is as good as making poor decisions – or worse. You can always go back and adjust a bad decision, but neglecting to move forward, because everyone is waiting on you, is a sure way to demotivate your team and show (through your "leadership") that it is OK to defer making tough choices. If this is the culture of the organization, it will be stuck in analysis paralysis, and is sure to crash and burn.

Implement Decisions: well
Of course, all your work is for naught if implementing your decisions (based on your prioritized, innovative solutions and known market need) is weak, poor or non-existent.

Again – if you do not have the skills, talent or desire to implement well, then find someone who does. This person should be a leader – to inspire, a manager – to deal with implementation issues, and should have experience in multiple levels within an organization as well as in different sized-companies / at different stages of their growth. In this way, you will be assured that s/he will not only be able to take your company to its next level, but its next several levels.

Non-linear approach to building your business
The diagram shown earlier implies a linear approach to building your company. This couldn't be further from the truth. Great companies are built on day to day decisions, which take into account changes in the market, competitors, new technologies, etc. And these change all the time. Therefore, a more-representative picture of the process is an iterative one: Where the market is reassessed, as are your ideas and decisions.

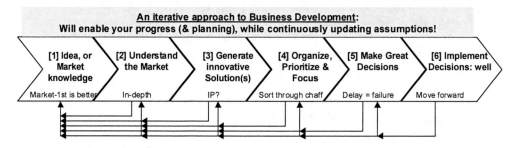

If you are looking to build a high-growth, lasting company that redefines the state of the art in a particular market, then ensure you or other members of your team have what it takes to address at least these six elements – defined in this chapter.

Raising Money in a Tight Market
(a.k.a. The Value of Bootstrapping)

With Sarbanes-Oxley requirements, volatile stock markets, private equity concerned about asset depreciation ("The Great Recession"), unemployment high, and investment money difficult to find, how can a going concern - let alone a start-up - raise money? What are investors looking for? How do you approach them? What do you have to say or do for them to part with their money and invest in *your* company?

Whatever you may think, investors are dealing with the same issues they have before: a unique opportunity, significant market size and growth, excellent management team, and a protectable & compelling solution. However, now they want to ensure they are not paying too much for your company, and are looking even harder at how and when you intend to generate profits. (Even with the recent actual or planned IPOs of LinkedIn, Pandora, Groupon & Facebook). Let's examine three critical elements to consider in today's economic environment.

✓ **Top-line.** Investors are acutely aware of the need to generate revenue. A lot of the companies that were funded from 1998 to 2001 were based on just an idea – taking new technology and applying it in new ways, with an eye on eventual revenue. Investors were looking for leverage, and paying a premium to potentially own a market space. Although there are still market-owning opportunities available, they are harder to find and fund. "Web 2.0" companies are being thought of as "Dot-bomb 2.0" by investors. We may be falling into the same trap, only 10 years later; LinkedIn aside. Pandora & Groupon are money-losing operations, yet considered going public.

Gerry Langeler, Partner at **OVP Venture Partners** with offices in the Portland, Oregon and Seattle, Washington areas, shared what he feels is the most important thing for CEOs to figure out when building their companies: "*Where does your idea fall among all the needs my customers have? Is it a 'must-have' or merely a 'nice to have'? If prospective customers can not tell you what they will cut back on or defer in order to squeeze you into their budget, you are not a must-have. VCs know that exciting top line growth comes from 'must-have' companies.*"

✓ **Bottom line.** It takes a lot of effort to go from having an idea, or identifying a market need, to *replicating a profit-generating business*. In fact, it is exactly the effort involved in moving from an idea to generating profits that lowers risk. Successfully executing a vision and making the difficult decisions on a daily basis are the very things investors find even more valuable now.

Kevin Gabelein, Managing Director at **Fluke Venture Partners** in Bellevue, Washington told me: "*Obviously, profitability is a much larger issue for investors now than a year ago. Investors are much more interested in proven and sustainable business models. Currently, the public markets are no longer interested in venture-funding companies with neat ideas and few customers. Each enterprise - with rare exception - will have to prove out the fundamentals under the VC's watch. Consequently, although deals are still being done, VCs are generally setting higher hurdles at the onset and demanding profitability within a shorter timeframe. Because the public markets are in turmoil and private equity is more difficult to obtain, there is higher financing risk associated with venture investments. Profitability within a reasonable timeframe is necessary if for no other reason than to ensure survivability during a risky financing climate.*"

✓ **Valuation.** From 1997 - 2001, and again in 2008 – 2010, broken asset bubbles shook the market. However, with LinkedIn IPO and others, the Next Big Thing is 'on' again. Since the IPO market is - in a word – 'variable' and liquidity events (or exit strategies) are murkier, it is more difficult to assess when Venture Capitalists will get their money out and provide a healthy return to *their* investors. Debi continues, "*There's been a sharp downturn in VC funding.*" Therefore, if you are interested in capturing the serious attention of angels or VCs, it is extremely important to be reasonable in how you value your company. Determine what you *need* to do to *win* and then gear what you are willing to accept around that. The investment game has changes from a seller's market to a buyer's market and back, often. Great team, with an identified market need, and a unique solution will still garner interest from investors – no matter the market.

Robert Campbell, Managing Director at **B | Riley Company** - an investment banking firm in Orange County, California provided this important insight regarding valuation: *"It is crucial to understand that the Internet bubble(s) in the financial markets are the exception, not the rule. Entrepreneurs cannot base their expectations or strategies on the hope that these high valuation conditions will return during their lifetime. Private equity investors' 'newfound' emphasis on profitable business models and traditional valuation parameters is only a return, after a very brief hiatus, to how this kind of investing has been done for the past 30 years."*

Another way to look at these issues is with the diagram on the following page. Obviously the process for building a business is more complex than this, but in terms of *where in the process* you can raise money, this chart is essential to understand.

Referring to the figure: Where are you in the capital-raising process? The earlier you are in the process, the higher the risk and lower the valuation. The later you are in the process, the lower the risk and higher the potential valuation. While raising money, your competition is not just the other company that will take sales from you, it is the previous and next business plans the investor will review. Your plan must provide a compelling story to the investor that your risk is lower, your company price is lower, your revenue upside higher, and that the probability of a win is excellent.

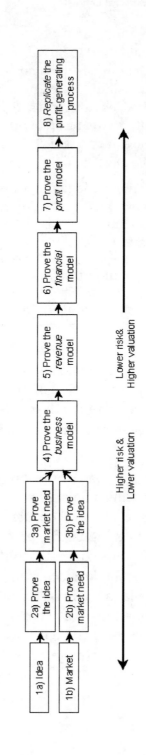

Figure 1: Business Development Flow

Another way to look at the challenge of raising money in today's "new-new economy" is to couple the diagram on the previous page with your High-Level Income Statement:

Figure 2: **High-level Income Statement**	
A) Gross Revenue	100%
B) Costs	
B1) Goods	X% (of revenue)
B2) Sales	Y%
B3) Marketing	Z%
B4) G&A	A%
B5) Development / engineering	B%
C) EBITDA*	C%

*Earnings before Interest, Taxes , Depreciation and Amortization

Step 1a) *Idea* and 1b) *Market* in the Business Development Flow (figure 1) above equates to B5) *Development / engineering* and B3) *Marketing* in the High-Level Income Statement (figure 2). As you move *further* along the Business Development Flow, you move *up* the Income Statement. Step 8) *Replicate a profit-generating process* equates to B2) *Cost of Sales* for service and B1) *Cost of Goods* for products. Imagine asking someone to invest $5 so you can generate $15 instead of investing just to prove your great idea. The probability of investment increases dramatically, and the value you get for your company also increases.

Wayne Embree, (ex-)Managing Partner at Reference Capital Management, LLC in Portland, Oregon – now at i2E, Inc. sums it up well: *"Down markets heighten investors' sense of risk. Their willingness to 'suspend disbelief' becomes greatly tempered. Although investors still have money, the fundamentals become all the more important. The team is more critical than usual because you don't get second chances. The product must be more tangible, if not ready for the market - unless the 'secret sauce' or 'magic' technology is so compelling that even a down market is irrelevant. If you really believe this is a great time to start a company, you should get rigorously honest about the team, the technology, and the product. And make absolutely certain you've done primary market analysis, spoken to real customers and understand who will buy, why they will buy and how they will buy. You must be honest, practical, pragmatic and articulate."*

The closer you can get your business to proving the bottom line, the higher the probability of getting funded. If you are seeking ways to increase the value of your company, obtain investment capital sooner, and build your company then you must figure out [1] how to acquire one customer, [2] how much they will pay for your product or service, [3] how much it takes to acquire that customer and then [4] how to efficiently replicate this process -- one customer at a time.

A final note: What is essential now, more than ever, is to prove to yourself that you can make money, first. Go sell something. Or at least try. If you can sell something (even a concept; where you get "in-industry" pre-sale interest or revenue), your business plan will shrink to just a couple pages: Your story changes to "This is how we are making money." Instead of how you are *going* to make money." If you can't sell anything, then why will anyone fund you?

Building Your Game Plan

So you have a great new idea to sell bazillions of new widgets, bring in a 95% gross margin and blow away the competition. All you need is a couple hundred thousand dollars. Shouldn't take too long, right? Think again. VCs (Venture Capitalists) and angel investors see thousands of business plans that profess the same thing, yet only an estimated two to five percent actually get funded. And of those, even fewer "make it". Why don't the rest? What is so special about the ones that do get funded?

Whether you are thinking about starting a new company or taking your current company to the next level of growth, there are several considerations to think about. Raising money is just one of them. Making sure the market is real and you have a business model to ensure your success won't ensure your success in raising the money you need. Thinking through and communicating specifically *how* you plan to overcome challenges better than *any* other company is your first objective, and raising money is second.

There are several aspects of a business that must be considered when starting or building your company. Not understanding these, nor dealing with them, will cost you time, money, and perhaps your company. The primary elements of a successful business (and therefore business plan) are:

✓ **Opportunity**: What trends or business changes are occurring? Why do you consider this a great *business* opportunity? What is the (identified and quantified) need that your idea addresses? What is your business model, and why will it outperform others? What does the return on investment look like? Is the return huge, or is it a niche market? If there is potential for a huge return, what if a Fortune 500 company decides to enter the same market? What is your sustainable competitive advantage and unique selling proposition?

✓ **Market**: What is going on in the market that supports your assertion of a new opportunity? What is the size of the market (the number of potential customers compared to the amount of money they will spend on your products / services)? How fast is the market growing? How are your potential customers *currently* satisfying their needs? *How have you validated this?* What are the niches that you will address first? Have you performed sufficient market research and documented your findings & determined the answers statistically?

✓ **Product / service**: What products or services do you plan to sell? What positioning are you going to have? Why? Have you thought through how each product will grow into an evolving product line, so that you have a *company* based on a series of ever-more valuable products and services? Or do you have a one-product concept?

✓ **Management**: Think about the functions needed in your company. What organizational holes exist? How are you going to fill them, while still making payroll? As the founder, do you feel you need to *always* be president? Will you be able to hand over control? Have you performed a realistic self-assessment of your *own* strengths and weaknesses?

✓ **Competition**: Do you know who, or what else will provides alternatives to your offering? Do you know details of their offering(s), so you can deliver even more value? Do you know their development plans and management strengths and weaknesses, so you can position your company and offerings accordingly?

✓ **Pricing**: Have you performed the necessary primary research to validate each product's value? (See "How to Maximize Revenue".)

✓ **Uniqueness**: What makes your offering stand out? Why is it the best, or most unique, or most valuable to your potential customers? Why will customers buy from you instead of competitors over the long haul? Do you have or can you get patents and trademarks to ensure you are protected from competitors and potential acquirers?

✓ **Leadership**: Who has the vision? If it's you, are you a "people person" who can clearly convey the vision and build the necessary team? How charismatic are you? Can you sell your idea, vision, opportunity, product, *and equity* in the company? Are you both adaptive to new scenarios *and* solid enough to stay the course, regardless of the roadblocks? Are you willing to mortgage your house to invest in the idea? What are your personal desires and motivations for this venture? What do you want in return? Are you willing to give up control to *win*?

✓ **Your team**: Do you have a team that supports your vision and the functions you will need to cover? How seasoned are they? How entrepreneurial and dedicated are they? Do your employees possess the talents you need? Do they have complementary talents and experiences? How much small *and* big business experience do they have? Will they stay the course with you?

✓ **Capital**: How much do you really need? What if things go wrong? What is the realistic return on investment? What assumptions have you made? What risks exist? How do you plan to mitigate these risks and what will these mitigation plans cost? Are you overly optimistic? Or pessimistic? In addition to your projected income, have you sorted through your projected profit and loss, and all-important cash flow? What are your exit strategies?

If the elements covered above are not considered thoroughly, thinking through the following elements will probably be a waste of time. Although these next elements come second, they are still extremely important to successfully launching a new business or in trying to take your company to its next level. Secondary elements of a successful business are:

✓ **Game Plan**: Now that you have thought through the issues stated above, it is time to put your thoughts into written plans. Most people think all they need is a Business Plan. What about your long term vision? Have you developed a Strategic Plan? On the other end of the spectrum, have you considered near-term tactics and developed your specific marketing and sales plans? Have you thought through - and proven(.) - all the ways to cost-effectively reach your best potential customers? Who are you going to joint venture with? Who will your strategic partners be? Why?

✓ **Distribution**: How do you plan on getting your product to market? Believing in "build it and they will come" is a sure path to failure. Understanding your customers' needs, how they buy, and why they make the decisions they do is critical to the success of your enterprise. Getting product to market is typically the least carefully thought about aspect of business development. Are you going direct? Why? Why not? What value do distributors, resellers, and dealers provide? Is it worth it? Are there alternate ways to reach the market?

✓ **Competition**: If this is such a great opportunity, why are others not already doing this? If there are competitors, who are they, what are they doing, and why will your offering be the best? Are you competing on price or performance or both? Stating "we have no competitors" is a red flag to investors and a sign that you do not really understand the market. How can your offering stand out from the crowd, and define a value that causes customers to flock to your door?

✓ **Sales and the sales process**: Who are you trying to reach? Does your service require field sales people or telesales or value-added resellers or order-takers or a unique way to sell? What do your customers read / listen to / view / already buy? What methods will you employ to reach them? Do you have a repeatable process or are you relying on your sales folk's charm and wit? Can you standardize the process? What tools are you going to use? How can you sell even more products and services into your existing customer base?

✓ **Financial model**: Is your financial model based on your vision, industry, market, and game plan to acquire revenue? Does it take risks into account? Anyone can develop a multi-page spreadsheet that is based on guesswork, and top-down assumptions. Does your model focus on what it takes to make just one sale, and then integrate that sale with the rest of the business assumptions, so that you have a realistic path to revenue? Are expenses in line with revenue-generation? Does your model allow for rapid scaling?

✓ **Organizational growth map**: What functions will be needed and when? Who is needed to fill open slots as you grow? How will you find people to fill them? What synergistic capabilities will you need? Do you have an HR (Human Resources) plan in place? Do you know what your compensation model is, how to reward performance, and how to deal with government laws, rules and regulations?

Once the issues above have been dealt with, there are other elements, which need to be addressed at some level:

✓ **Your non-management team**: In addition to your management team, hiring exceptional people will make an incredible difference in both your top line and bottom line. Do you know who you are going to need? What is your company's hire and fire process? Do you have position descriptions and career-paths in place? If not, when will you need them, both to grow and to minimize potential liability?

✓ **Success processes**: How are you going to ensure success now *and* in the future? How will you reward personal and organizational performance? What succession planning have you done? Who will take over for you when you move on? Do you *want* to lead and are you *capable* of leading a much larger organization? As the market changes and competition erodes your positioning, how are you going to adapt and leapfrog your competitors?

Your chances of success increase greatly by codifying the elements stated above into an executive summary, business plan, necessary attachments and presentation (see "Building Your Story").

Obviously, there are myriad issues to deal with, whether you are trying to start a company or bring your company to its next level. Your success in reaching your desired level of growth depends on how you approach these issues. After that, the market and opportunity (or lack thereof) will deliver the answer loud and clear.

Building Your Team

When you think of your company's team, who comes to mind? You? Your senior managers? Your employees? Project teams? As president or CEO of your company, you can cost-effectively add incredible talent to your team. By emulating large companies, you will have a better chance of obtaining their success. And without spending a fortune, your company could break through its current performance and attain the next level of growth - *if* the support you need is in place.

In addition to ensuring a real market has been defined and quantified, building your management team is the most important action you can take – whether you are a CEO hiring your CMO, or a CIO hiring your Director of Information Technology. Finding the right people that fit with your market, technology - and your leadership style, and those who will take significant actions to help you accomplish your game plan - is required to find funding and/or build the company.

For a going concern, please see "How to hire the best", and do not hesitate to hire a qualified search firm. For the entrepreneur, this task may seem like a conundrum: no funding to hire management and no management to attract funding. This enigma can be solved in various ways. The most common way is to network. Industry association events are an excellent way to meet people within your industry, as is LinkedIn.com. Someone usually knows someone else who may be able to add incredible value to your operations.

Talking with bankers, lawyers, accountants, consultants, venture capitalists, and other entrepreneurs will lead you to like-minded people. You do not always need funding to attract excellent executives. A proven market need, a significantly unique solution, and an opportunity to make a real difference in the world (like renewable energy) might be all you need to have someone allow you to use their resume/bio in confidence to continue your fund-raising.

Additionally, think outside your current team. Look to outside sources for advice, counsel and expertise. These people will not add to your payroll, yet they provide tremendous benefits to you, your employees, customers, and stockholders.

There are three "teams" that entrepreneurs of smaller companies tend to underestimate, who can add significant value to their enterprise and help the company attain its goals. Ideally, these teams need to be in place from the very start. The three teams to seriously consider are:

✓ **Board of Directors**: The directors' fiduciary responsibilities to the stockholders include - ensuring the right CEO is in place and maximizing long-term shareholder value. The Board can provide significant advice and counsel to the CEO, to ensure appropriate executive compensation and that good operating plans are in place, and administer stock option plans, ensure formal audits occur. Most importantly, they can be a sounding board for new ideas and overcoming challenging problems. Especially if you're open to their ideas.

For small to mid-sized companies, in which the CEO is the founder (and for many high-tech companies, the technical expert as well), "to ensure the right CEO is in place" may sound scary. If you think about it, this is exactly what you want the board to do. If for some reason you have skills, which would be far better used in a different role in the company, then you should seriously consider that new role. Many smaller companies have "founder's syndrome." (Otherwise known as "Founderitis".) The owner wants to run everything, even though more qualified people are available. Typically, management, operations, sales, marketing, and business development experience is what is needed to get a company to the next level. As long as revenue, profits and the value of your stockholders ownership go up, isn't that what is important? So allow the board to do its job.

✓ **Board of Advisors**: Advisors are much like a Board of Directors in terms of providing advice and counsel, but they don't have the same fiduciary responsibilities. Use an advisory board to add functional expertise, industry experts and contacts that might be able to provide critical insights on an on-going basis.

✓ **Strategic Partners**: If you add these critical partners to your team and listen to their advice, you will be miles ahead. These partners are a law firm, an accounting firm, a banking partner, and even consultants. These partners should be chosen carefully and with skillful purpose. Don't look at their bill rates or loan rates as deciding factors. Review their areas of expertise, the value they can bring immediately and in the long run, and their personality compatibility. You want a team that is focused on your company's success, not just someone to do taxes, handle a contract, or provide a loan. Ad agencies, PR firms and consultancies can also add significant value to your company. Additionally, suppliers, distributors and others can support you via good will, or help you market and sell your products. What you are seeking is leverage in the marketplace. If you chose excellent partners, the rewards to your company can be tremendous. Just imagine the value of your business if a potential supplier invested in your company. You would be able to attract more investors and / or customers.

Although most companies have a lawyer, accountant, and banker, are they really *team members* or just people who do work for you and collect fees? Have you asked them for advice and allowed them to support you in other ways? For instance, a banker can assist you in many ways, reviewing your business plan, and introducing you to potential strategic partners and senior management talent who could help you set and achieve aggressive goals.

Building a Board of Directors/Advisors:

You will want to balance the makeup of the Board of Directors or Advisors in a way that optimizes your ability to successfully compete in a rapidly changing environment. The makeup may include:

[1] People with connections to money (Angels, VCs, Investment Banking) or strategic partners

[2] Investors,

[3] People with specific industry expertise,

[4] "Been there / done that" types of people who have experienced the growth cycle you are planning for your company.

All are important and should be considered when establishing boards. When building your board, you might consider temporary support from trusted, well-known consultants. Those in particular areas of specialty can help you attract new outside members that can support your growth objectives. Once the board is built, the temporary members would then move on – especially for advisors. Avoid using friends and family. You want impartial advice and counsel, and you want to escape the pitfalls of family-oriented, emotionally charged meetings.

Additionally, you will want to consider the following functional areas when building boards: General Management, Marketing and Sales, Operations, Finance, Legal, and Human Resources. Senior executives, especially those, who have significant experience, can save valuable time and money in helping you set and achieve aggressive goals. Experienced consultants can also help you.

How to make it happen:

Finding accountants, lawyers, bankers and consultants: There are many credible service providers available. Take the time to interview them carefully, and you will be able to find the right team members: Through the web or your regional yellow pages, search for associations in your field. Or get in touch with your local Chamber of Commerce, or find other entrepreneurs in your industry and learn what they have learned. Do they have a long list of satisfied clients? Do they have testimonials stating this?

Finding Board Members: Of course, the easiest way it to find candidates is to talk with your lawyer, accountant and banker. They can identify candidates, but you will have to determine the mix you think you need. Through meeting and interviewing these candidates, you will obtain the information you need to make decisions on who to bring on board.

Motivating them to come on board:

One way to bring experienced talent onto your team is to provide stock or stock options, depending on your organizational form, tax issues, and your particular situation. Agreements can be worked out... That is the easy part. Building and using your team to its full potential and reaping its rewards takes time, so get going. Take that first step now to dramatic improvement - and build the team that will take your company to its next level.

Sidebar: Responsibilities of a Board of Directors:

Fiduciary Responsibilities:

1) <u>Make sure the right CEO is in place</u>: Perform the hiring and firing of the company's leader. Unless the right leader and team are in place, the other objectives of the company are not going to happen.

2) <u>Maximize long term shareholder value</u>: In the case of a floundering company, maximize enterprise value as there may be nothing left for shareholders after the secured and unsecured creditors get their due. Ensuring the right management team is in place is the first step in maximizing enterprise value.

Operational Functions:

1) <u>Ensure good operating plans are in place</u>: The discipline from a Board that requires this is often very helpful to a small company that may be so focused on day-to-day survival that they do not look forward far enough. A Business Plan and annual department budgets are mandatory. Department operating plans help connect all the operating groups with

the strategic vision of the company. The Business Plan needs to contain objectives, strategies to meet objectives, specific tactics, and full financials. Comparing these budget projections versus actual financial reports becomes part of the discussions at the Board's meetings.

The operating plan raises another key question. Is the company adequately capitalized? If the revenue plan is missed, is there an adequate cash and credit buffer? If growth exceeds expectations, can this be funded? Are there contingency plans to adjust tactics or expenses if the plan is being missed? For example, a Board may find itself helping manage profit expectations down for several years by investing in R&D at the expense of double-digit profits, with the expectation that this investment will pay off later. An independent and impartial Board often helps this type of discussion and strategic thinking.

2) Compensation committee: Is the executive team appropriately compensated based on the industry and the competitive environment for good people? It is impossible to keep a good management team if the incentives are too low. However, maximizing enterprise value means they should not be over-compensated. What is the mix of salary versus incentive based on cash or stock bonuses? What are the qualitative or quantitative milestones on which incentives are based? Management is not in a position to impartially set their own compensation in a way that would meet the acceptance of all outside investors and shareholders.

3) Administer stock option pool: Ensure there is a clear and consistent program to grant options. Another important Board responsibility is setting the fair market value of the stock which may have to stand up to IRS scrutiny. You often

want it as low as possible so you can get stock into employee's hands at a low price. However, it must be at a level commensurate with the market value and associated risk and liquidity. The board needs to use a gradually evolving formula that is *consistently* applied.

4) Formal audits: As a company gets larger and begins to look to the capital markets, a formal audit committee of outside Board members can ensure that appropriate financial and HR policies and procedures are in place, and that they will withstand outside scrutiny.

5) Sounding board: Finally, a good Board provides valuable, independent advice on many issues. It is always helpful to have a good sounding board to help with major decisions. Boards help with interviewing key hires (VP Marketing/Sales, etc.), evaluating acquisition targets, facilitating merger discussions, evaluating long term strategies, etc. If the Board is structured correctly, a group of very valuable consultants can be brought onto the existing company team, often for stock options. Their sense of ownership and responsibility will encourage them to make every effort to help the company become successful.

6) Frequency of meetings: Typically, Board meetings are held quarterly, unless business conditions warrant otherwise. Usually meetings are held more frequently at the beginning stages of a company, or in companies dealing with rapidly changing business environments.

Building Your Story

Many entrepreneurs feel that raising money is all that is needed. *"All I need is $250,000 to make this company work."* and *"Do you know where I can get investors who will fund this idea?"* Or *"What's wrong with those VC's? Don't they know a great idea when they see one? All I'm asking for is $6 million, which will make them $60 million."*

There are several things you, as the leader, *must* do in order to convince investors to invest in your vision. First of all, build your management team, Board of Directors, Board of Advisors, and outside team. "Selling" your idea or business vision to others (and having them buy in.) provides great third-party credibility. Another critical element needed to successfully raise money is your "story," which you *must* have before you can successfully convince investors to part with *their* hard-earned capital.

Your story is key to your success.

As the CEO, it is critical that you can share your vision with potential investors and even potential employees with enthusiasm, clarity and brevity.

What are the top issues – besides return on investment – which will catch an investor's attention? They are interested in opportunity, market size and growth rate, the people on the management team, your solutions, why there is a sustainable competitive advantage, what your sales, profits and cash flow will be, and so on.

The most important thing to remember is that you are not trying to get the investor to write the check right then and there. You are trying to get feedback on their level of interest. *You must first sell the meeting to present your venture.*

Before you talk with investors, it is very important to obtain feedback from people who can help you improve your concept, pitch and approach. You have one real shot at investors when asking them to invest, so ensure your story is well critiqued by others. One way is to develop a 10 to 12 sheet presentation with salient points. Use this rough presentation as an outline to share your vision with others. Set up meetings with bankers, lawyers and accountants to "pitch" your idea and listen intently to their questions. If you do this 20 to 30 times in one-on-one meetings – updating your pitch every time – you will soon find your concept shifting due to great feedback. If your vision still seems viable, you will need to develop your business plan in sufficient detail to address investors' concerns. You can then use the plan to build your elevator pitch and update your presentation.

✓ **Elevator pitch:** Actually, there are at least two "pitches." The first is a one or two sentence description of your venture. This is very difficult, but essential to conveying to the listener what you are all about. (As if you meet that important person in an elevator who you've been trying to contact and need to convey your idea in 15 seconds) If they show interest, then you can proceed to the 1 to 2 minute explanation and then, if they continue to listen intently, to the 6 to 10 minute version. *The pitch's purpose is to generate enough interest so they invite you to give your presentation. It is not to do a data dump of everything you know and love about your idea, product or service.*

✓ **Presentation:** Once you have been invited to present your business idea, then be prepared to share the pertinent information *in which the investor is interested.* It is not just about your product. It is about your customers (first) then your business - how to plan on generating a growing, profitable business. Why? Because it is about return on *their* investment.

The presentation should be between 5 and 15 minutes long, depending on the forum and how much time you have been given, so be prepared to cut to the chase. If you respect the investor's time (and show it), they will respect you. *The purpose of the presentation is not to tell the investor everything you know about the product. It is to convey the most fundamental insights into why there is a unique and **real** opportunity for them, and to show that you have assembled the right team to make that opportunity a reality.*

✓ **Business plan:** Many will tell you that in Internet-time (or now... *"Web 2.0 time"*), there is no time to write a business plan. Although this may be acceptable in only a few situations, you still have to do your homework. You will have to understand customers, the market, competition, unique selling proposition, revenue model, etc., and be able to convey this information crisply. If at all possible, make the executive summary one page and the business plan as short as possible (8 to 12 pages). Put additional back-up information into an attachment. Although this is a real test of your communication skills, your *current* competition is the previous and the next business plans the investor sees. *The purpose of your plan is not to get the investor to write the check, but for them to know you have done your homework and that perhaps, just perhaps, it might be worth their time to consider investing in your company seriously.* Make it easy for them.

✓ **Your personal style:** The manner in which you present your concept speaks volumes about what kind of partner you will be if investors fund your company. Do you get to the point? Are you confident, while not being defensive? Do you have infectious enthusiasm? Do you provide a 30,000-foot view and avoid a "data dump"? Are you organized, succinct and mindful of the investor's time? Do you listen? Are you open to suggestions - or are you defensive? *You* are the most important factor - as to why an investor will even listen to the rest of your pitch. Most entrepreneurs don't see this.

Do you need help? If the investors tell you to "get an advisory board," they are probably telling you that you have not convinced them that there is a real opportunity. Or that you do not have the management / leadership talent on your team necessary to capitalize on the opportunity. Or your story was not convincing.

As the CEO, your role is to *share the vision, build the team, and find the resources* to make the vision come true. (And some say *"Get out of the way."*) Communicate your idea clearly and concisely, so that your entire team, including the investor, is driving towards identifiable objectives.

Is this all there is to it? Of course not. Things like having customers, not overvaluing your company, and being flexible with your role as the leader are also essential for success. But your team will help you with your story, and you need a great story to build your team. (Yes, it is iterative.) Out of the hundreds of ideas investors see every year, only a few get funded. To get your idea to the top of the heap, make sure it enters near the top, using your *entire* team, and make sure it stays at the top with an exceptionally clear story that conveys why your idea will make the investor even wealthier.

Creating Your Stock Structure

When looking for equity financing, entrepreneurs want to know how much of the company they should give up, and when? What happens when they lose control? How do they know how much money to raise? When will they need financing? How do investors get their money back? How much will the stock be worth... and when?"

A well thought out business plan, with accompanying financials, will answer most of these questions. However, an often-overlooked piece of the puzzle is the corporate stock structure: how to create a clear road map for stockholders and help guide your funding decisions.

Communication is critical: When you are looking for investment capital, the more easily you can show *how* and *when* investors will make money, the easier it will be for you to obtain funding. In the next few paragraphs, you will learn how to clearly and concisely develop and communicate just one aspect of your company's growth in value. The spreadsheet on page 79 is provided for your review as you read this chapter.

Three caveats: [1] The example provided in the spreadsheet[3] is to give you a very rough idea of what to consider – it is *not* to be used as the defacto approach you should take. [2] This example is especially applicable if you are considering going public, although you will gain insights to help guide you as you are getting your company ready for its next level.

[3] Make sure you work with your lawyer and accountant in putting your corporate structure together.

To more easily understand the basics of offering stock, let's start at the end and work backwards:

- ✓ **Liquidity event:** Determine how much money you will need at your company's sale, or the Initial Public Offering* (IPO) to implement your plan and therefore how *many shares your company will need* when you go public (at about $10 to $15 a share). This is a key number based on market size, growth rate, and your business model to acquire market share. Market capitalization is determined by many factors, but remember, this is just a model to help guide you. In the example, you are raising $50 million by selling 5 million shares.

- ✓ **Prior to IPO:** Before you go public, chances are you will have a second venture capital or mezzanine round. In this example's round, you might expect to raise about $15 million at $2 to $3 a share. You will need about 5 million shares.

- ✓ **First VC round:** Before you seek your second VC round and after you successfully raise angel financing and prove the business model, you may well seek initial VC financing. Expect to pay a premium for this round, because it is the first professional, or institutional infusion of money, which will undoubtedly require that you actually agree to accept vesting in your own stock. At this stage, you might raise $5 to $10 million at around $1 per share. You will need between 5 to 10 million shares.

* I am using the "Initial Public Offering" purely as an example. Most companies will never go public. If you think your will and that it is a foregone conclusion, rest assured, this will not likely happen. Please use "IPO" as a *placeholder* for your final exit. It is far likelier that you will get acquired, though this is also rare. The template is just that – a way to visualize your company's future... in terms of liquidity – that investors will look for. If this won't happen, don't look to raise money, unless from very specific individual investors who are in your industry and who can benefit from cash flow.

✓ **First angel round:** If you have a great idea (or better yet, an actual product or service and a proven market), you may need angel financing to get your venture off the ground. In this case, you will pay the dearest price for investment capital. However, this kind of financing represents the highest risk, too. For this example, you might raise $500,000 to $1 million at 40 to 60 cents per share. This will require around two million shares.

✓ **Building your management team:** Before you can seriously seek angel financing, your management team, Board of Advisors and Board of Directors will need to be in place. You will also need to reserve stock options for future employees, as well as future management. A twenty-reserve is the minimum at this stage. If you are looking for venture capital money, VCs will require more. Once your team is in place, your company might be worth 10 to 50 cents a share, depending on several factors that are outside the context of this chapter.

✓ **Your stock, as founder:** When you first have the idea, your company's par value may be worth between 0 to 50 cents a share. Many entrepreneurs feel their company is worth $5 to $15 million in market capitalization from the get-go. Do not make this mistake, unless you want to be in fund-raising mode the rest of your life. Based on the investment steps prior to IPO, you can start gaining an idea of how many shares you and your team will need to fit into the profile outlined in the spreadsheet. With these insights, you'll be in a much better position to know how much of the company you will own, and when. As you can see in this example, starting off with about 3 million issued shares (and about 10 to 30 million authorized shares) will make the model work.

So what does all this mean? As long as the value of your stock continues to increase, it should not matter if you give up control of the company. If your investors win, you win. As long as you are more interested in having your company succeed than in retaining ownership, you will be in a far better position to get funding.

Let's take a look at the example and what it means to the entrepreneur:

Event:	CEO Ownership	Price per share		Value of CEO stock	
Creation	100.00%	$	0.10	$	305,000
Build team	30.50%	$	0.20	$	610,000
Angel round	24.40%	$	0.35	$	1,067,500
1st VC round	18.48%	$	1.00	$	3,050,000
2nd VC round	15.48%	$	2.50	$	7,625,000
IPO	12.87%	$	7.50	$	22,875,000

Company ABC: Corporate Growth Strategy

Stage 0

		# of shares
CEO	100%	3,050,000
Total Company:	100%	3,050,000
Amount invested:		
Total shares:		3,050,000
Price per share:	$	0.10
Valuation:	$	305,000
Total ownership (check):	100%	

Stage 1: Mnmngt team on board

		# of shares
CEO	31%	3,050,000
Management Team	46%	4,625,000
Employees / reserve	20%	2,000,000
Board of Advrs/Drctrs	3%	325,000
Total Company:	100%	10,000,000
Angel round:		
Amount invested:		
Total shares:		10,000,000
Price per share:	$	0.20
Valuation:	$	2,000,000
Total ownership (check):	100%	

Stage 2: Angels on board

		# of shares		# of shares
CEO	24.40%	3,050,000		3,050,000
Management Team	37.00%	4,625,000		4,625,000
Employees / reserve	16.00%	2,000,000		2,000,000
Board of Advrs/Drctrs	2.60%	325,000		325,000
Total Company:	80%	10,000,000		10,000,000
Angel round:	20%	2,500,000		2,500,000
Amount invested:			$	875,000
Total shares:				12,500,000
Price per share:			$	0.35
Valuation:			$	4,375,000
Total ownership:	100%			

The 'chasm' for the entrepreneur →

Stage 3: VC on board

		# of shares
CEO	18.48%	3,050,000
Management Team	28.03%	4,625,000
Employees / reserve	12.12%	2,000,000
Board of Directors	1.97%	325,000
Total Company:	60.61%	10,000,000
Angel round:	15.15%	2,500,000
VC 1st round:	24.24%	4,000,000
Total ownership:	100%	
Amount invested:	$	4,000,000
Total shares:		16,500,000
Price per share:	$	1.00
Valuation:	$	16,500,000

Stage 4: 2nd VC round

		# of shares
CEO	15.48%	3,050,000
Management Team	23.48%	4,625,000
Employees / reserve	10.15%	2,000,000
Board of Directors	1.65%	325,000
Total Company:	50.76%	10,000,000
Angel round:	12.69%	2,500,000
VC 1st round:	20.30%	4,000,000
VC 2nd round:	16.24%	3,200,000
Total ownership:	100%	
Amount invested:	$	8,000,000
Total shares:		19,700,000
Price per share:	$	2.50
Valuation:	$	49,250,000

Stage 5: Acquisition / IPO

		# of shares	Value after public:	At $50 a share
CEO	12.87%	3,050,000	$ 22,875,000	$ 114,375,000
Management Team	19.51%	4,625,000	$ 34,687,500	$ 173,437,500
Employees / reserve	8.44%	2,000,000	$ 15,000,000	$ 75,000,000
Board of Directors	1.37%	325,000	$ 2,437,500	$ 12,187,500
Total Company:	42.19%	10,000,000	$ 75,000,000	$ 375,000,000
Angel round:	10.55%	2,500,000	$ 18,750,000	$ 93,750,000
VC 1st round:	16.88%	4,000,000	$ 30,000,000	$ 150,000,000
VC 2nd round:	13.50%	3,200,000	$ 24,000,000	$ 120,000,000
Acquisition / IPO:	16.88%	4,000,000	$ 30,000,000	$ 150,000,000
	100%			
Amount invested:	$	30,000,000		
Total shares:		23,700,000		
Price per share:	$	7.50		
Valuation:	$	177,750,000		

It is important to realize that this is *just an example* to encourage you to ponder what it might take to build a company that rewards all participants

Building Credibility

As the founding entrepreneur for your start-up company, you have plenty to worry about. Building your team, creating your business plan, and raising financing are all critical to your success. If you have an unproven concept, how do you get anyone to buy in? How do you increase your chances of funding? How do you minimize the amount of the company you need to sell for equity?

Third party credibility is essential to raising money

Telling everyone how great your idea is offers one level of believability. Having others tell them offers a higher level. Having customers tell your investors to fund your company builds your case better than you ever could. So how do you go about getting customers when you do not even have a product or service?

Seed funding

Defining your prospective customers' needs is the single-most important thing to do. Having a defined market need is essential to raise capital. But this is certainly not all that is required. A few tips on how to build your company's credibility and support your fund-raising efforts:

The tip that could save your company

Before you have something tangible to offer customers, you have your word. More importantly, you have your ears. If you can structure the appropriate customer research, you can fashion your offerings so customers are more compelled to buy. Why? With an intense focus on your product or service - instead of customers' quantified needs - you may alienate investors and not even know it.

There are at least three areas of research you will need to conduct to build the *right* product or service and to raise the capital you need:

✓ **End users:** Find out if they will buy what you are offering. Through a process described in another chapter in the Entrepreneur's Survival Guide, *"How to Value-Price Your Products and Services"*, you will not only determine the customers' desire for what you are selling, you will also be able to increase the product's value by adding specific features they say they will pay (more) for and delete features they will not. Through a repeatable process, you can obtain invaluable customer feedback to guide your product development. With research results, you will be able to show potential investors what customers think before you even spend a dime developing your idea.

✓ **Strategic Partners:** Whether you are developing a product that requires vendors for manufacturing or services in which partners receive remuneration for their participation, you can determine exactly how valuable your new company will be to them. You will need to be clear on what you are offering and you will need to be able to write, with help from your lawyer, an LOI (Letter of Intent). Armed with the LOI, *try to sell something* to potential customers or partners and find out their objections. Until you ask someone to sign their name on a piece of paper, you will not really know their specific reasons for buying - or not buying.

Once you get one LOI signed, write even more specific terms, increasing the price or percentages in your favor, until you are turned down. It is only at this point that you know your terms are unrealistic. Then back down a notch or two and get as many signed LOI's as you need in order to prove your concept. Of course, signed contracts are even better. These relationships are extremely important and may mean the difference between getting funded or not.

✓ **Competitive assessment:** This is especially valid if you have a beta version of your product. Get someone to test your product against those you feel will create the greatest competitive threat. Develop quantitative and qualitative assessments, which will show you and potential investors how your offering stands up against others in the field. If this assessment shows you have a real winner, great. If not, you will need to adjust features and functions accordingly, until it comes out on top. (Or you can take the low-price/low quality niche.) Independent labs can do a great job at this, as can colleges and universities.

VC Funding

Moving your company to its next level requires additional credibility and validation in the form of:

✓ Showing early evidence that your plan is being executed and generating revenue as anticipated.

✓ Having successful pilot customers who will vouch for the value of your solution.

✓ Paying customers.

✓ Early strategic partnerships and alliances.

✓ Negotiated partnerships with distributors, channel partners and others to help your product get to market.

✓ LOIs from large (or many) potential customers.

✓ Positive press from industry associations and analysts.

Third party credibility can provide the lift your company needs

By lining up potential customers and strategic partners, and knowing what they want before you start seeking funding - or bootstrapping your company - you will dramatically increase your company's probability of success.

Knowing how your offerings compare against the leading contenders' will favorably position you as you raise money. And it will lower how much of your company you will need to exchange for equity financing - due to lowered risk. In fact, if you follow this course, you may even find customer financing for your venture. If what you have to offer is valuable to your strategic partners, they may well provide the seed financing you need.

The Realities of Raising Money

You have a great product idea, and you have done careful market research. There is a huge demand for your idea, your business plan is done, you have demonstrated early market validation, and you are ready to raise that million and a half so you can implement your plan.

Because of the detailed analyses you have conducted and the contacts you have made, you plan on closing your funding in three months and are doing much better than your conservative plan showed. Initial responses have all been very favorable, you have some initial press, and things are looking up. All you need is to convince a few folks how great your plan is, and that million and a half dollars are yours. It is not as easy as you might think. Here are the usual problems to consider when trying to raise money:

Credible business plan: Does your plan address the opportunity, market size and growth, specific need for the product or service, technical stumbling blocks, unique selling proposition, management expertise, financial projections and capital needs, and qualifications of your team? Beware of using catch phrases - like "This is a trillion dollar market... all we need is 10% of it." Or "We have no competition." Investors view them as red flags rather than assurances.

Your team's strengths & weaknesses: Have you made an honest assessment of your team? What is your plan for filling holes in your management team? Is it realistic? Do you have people on tap to address weaknesses? **Alan Dishlip,**

previously General Partner at **Utah Venture Partners,** insists success starts with leadership: *"A critical area I look at is management: Will the entrepreneur hire people who are smarter and better than they are and be able to turn over the reins if and when it's time? This is essential when building a management team."*

Beware the "dead zone": For various reasons, requests for less than $1,500,000 are typically better suited for angel investors, while venture capitalists (VC's) like to see the total of all rounds on the order of $3 to $6 million or more (although these ranges vary depending on equity markets and the economy). It is very difficult to raise capital between $1,500,000 and three million dollars. If your plan is in that zone, have a great exit strategy that allows investors to see how and when they will see a return on their investment.

Cash flow: Do not just estimate startup costs and ask for that amount. An assessment of cash flow based on real market size, how much revenue you will get as a result of the costs of implementing your business plan, and assumptions (like accounts-receivable aging and sales cycle) is the *only* real measure of your capital needs.

Time frame: Triple the amount of time you think you will need to raise the money. If you think you need four months, count on twelve. During this time you must survive on your own, and that is a great test to see if you can make decisions under real pressure. Raising money will take longer than you ever think it will; you can count on that. **Nancy Isely-Fletcher,** previously with **Coldstream Capital** in Seattle, asks the critical question, *"What if you can't get funding right away? Be prepared to cut back expenses to survive until the funding comes in. Don't wait until the last minute to go out for funding. You cannot rush the process."*

Researching Potential Investors: The research process of finding the right customers for your products is also valid in finding the right investors for your company. For seed capital, accountants, lawyers, bankers and consultants know people who might fit with your type of company and industry you are serving. With the web, you can quickly obtain information on venture capitalists, and determine the types of deals they are looking for, what industries they invest in, and what stage companies fit with their risk levels. If they are investing in a competing company, they might not be able to even talk with you. **Bill Kallman**, Founding Partner with **Timberline Ventures,** an information technology venture firm, says, *"Entrepreneurs definitely need to understand their target investors. If you're looking for a first round for a software company you should focus on investors who make that kind of investment versus a mezzanine round in another field, like biotech."*

Approaching Investors: Once you have filtered your initial list of 250+ potential investors to the most appropriate 10 to 20, determine a few specific companies in your industry they have invested in, and approach a senior executive for an informational interview (if the company is not a competitor). Share your vision and ask for feedback. If there seems to be a real synergy, the executive might offer to introduce you to a partner at a VC firm. Be kind with their time. "Investee's" executives are often on the lookout for great new ideas to feed to their investors. You may only have one shot, so be wise in your choices.

Evaluating Offers / Negotiating the Deal: Entire books have been written on this subject. Suffice to say, ensure you have a negotiating team together which includes your legal counsel.

Smart money: What qualifies the investor as someone who can provide more than just greenbacks? Will they provide strategic advice? Industry knowledge? Technology expertise? Contacts? Board member additions? It is essential that you develop a positive relationship with someone who has "been there/done that;" their advice may well save your company.

Your core values: Why is the investor interested in investing in your company? Is it just return on investment? What is their motivation for helping you? What can you both gain from a partnership? Are they interested in (just) a quick buck, or does this investment play with others they have in a symbiotic way, so that the value of their involvement is worth to all involved?

Buyer beware: Unfortunately, people are not always who they seem. A great deal now may be a lousy deal later. Is it worth giving up your dream to someone you do not really know? Perform reference checking to ensure you are getting a high quality partner. Whatever papers you sign can be renegotiated later. It happens all the time, for myriad reasons.

Your next move: You have your money, now what? What are your first moves, in relation to your plan? Are you going to follow the plan and your team's advice, or just spend money based on gut feel? Sure, you will need to be flexible and figure out market changes before your competition, but how you use the money speaks volumes about your ethics. Make sure you speak with integrity and directed purpose. These are just a few of the realities of raising money. There are hundreds of other subtle but extremely important issues you will need to deal with. Involve your entire team and use their advice. They will be able to help you through these, and hundreds more.

Section 3

Improving Marketing and Sales Performance

- **The Real Value of Market Research**
- **How to Value-Price Your Products and Services**
- **Maximizing Marketing ROI: Tying Research to Sales**
- **Strategic Selling Skills for Technology Entrepreneurs**
- **How to Attract Significantly More Customers**

The purpose of this section is to help the technically oriented entrepreneur better understand how to position their products and services for highest value, *as perceived by the customer*. It is difficult for some entrepreneurs to appreciate the need for and value of market research, the need for understanding customers' requirements *before* developing products, and how to then effectively sell their products and services. This section is intended to provide insights into a few tips and tricks to easily understand what customers want and how to better satisfy their needs.

The Real Value of Market Research

Time and again, business leaders tell me they know what is best for their customers. "Our customers aren't innovators. We have the technical talent to create products and services that our customers could never figure out. Why do we need market research?" Usually they continue, "We don't have time for market research, anyway. It costs too much, takes too long, and just confirms what we already know."

Michael Shenker, an independent sales and marketing consultant, sums it up. *"There is a word for starting a business or launching a new product without conducting market research...it's called suicide. Market research saves time, saves money, and optimizes the probability of success."*

If fear of extinction does not motivate you to talk with your existing and potential customers, please do not bother reading the rest of this chapter. If, however, you are interested in beating your competition and creating customers for life, then read on.

The question heard most often is "How do I find out what they want?" The answer lies in asking more specific questions:

✓ **Who are your best customers?** If you can learn which customers buy from you soonest, cost the least to attract, pay the most, refer others to you, and come back over and over, *those* are the customers you want. In terms of profitability, your best customers may be worth ten times your worst customers. Isn't your company worth the time and effort to find out? There are ways to determine who your best customers are, and it's through market research.

✓ **What do your customers want?** A fundamental understanding of your customers' needs is critical to your product and service development, your corporate positioning and your marketing strategy. Your offerings should both directly respond to what they need as well as lead the way – to new and more efficient solutions to their problems. These conflicting views provide the balance needed for innovation and competitive positioning. The "what" provides you what their tangible needs are.

✓ **Why do they buy?** Find their compelling reasons to purchase. What motivates them? What are their underlying reasons for buying a solution? How do you know? Finding out the answers, using an analytic method, instead of in anecdotal terms can yield significant insights as to what is driving your customers' behavior. The "why" provides you what their intangible needs are.

✓ **How do they buy?** Determine how potential customers obtain information about competing products and services. How do you plug into their purchasing process? If you're trying to sell at trade shows, and they buy because of PR, wouldn't it make sense to shift your budget accordingly?

✓ **How do they currently solve their problems?** If they already address their needs with superior, less expensive solutions, it's time to head back to the drawing board.

✓ **When do they buy?** Understanding customers' budgeting cycle can help you align your marketing tactics (i.e. expenses) with them, which will save you time and money.

✓ **What else do they buy, instead?** Understand who is competing against you, and why customers buy their products or services instead of yours.

Answers to these questions can be found through quantitative and qualitative questions of both customers and non-customers:

	Open ended phone surveys:	Closed-ended questionnaires
Customers:	Talk with your customers and find out why they bought your product or services from you instead of others.	Develop a questionnaire to determine why they bought from you. Ask specific questions about their needs.
Non-Customers:	Talk with your prospects and find out their needs in your area. If they are not buying, what will compel them to buy?	Develop a questionnaire and learn what they buy, why they buy, and how they buy. Ask specific questions about their needs.

It is important to use the information found during interviews and from questionnaires to find out how you can best use your scarce marketing and sales budget to target your customers' needs – in a much more efficient and effective manner.

Make sure your analysis provides you statistic on the answers, not just anecdotal information. Use Affinity Diagramming (Google it) to assess trends and extract information you can only find out through systematic market research and analysis. Responding to one *loud* customer can be misleading. Obtain a dozen responses at first, and more to see trends.

Depending on your budget, you can do the work yourself, hire a consulting firm or hire a market research firm. The benefits of finding your customers' specific needs and buying patterns far outweigh the costs involved to perform effective market research. Build your marketing research and turbo-charge your marketing strategy.

Then align your tactics with your strategies.

How to Value-Price Your Products and Services

This chapter addresses *one* method of maximizing revenue through value pricing and focuses on how to price your products and services.

How do you currently price products? Do you review your competitors' prices? Do you "cost out" your solution, then add a mark-up? Do you talk to a few customers and ask what they would be willing to pay?

The first two methods, though essential in understanding your competitive positioning, don't give you a true understanding of how customers will value your product or service. And the third method can yield misleading results. Often, *lower* than what the market will really bear.

And when do you figure out the price? *Before* you develop a product, or afterwards?

Many people say that marketing is an art, not a science, and that you have to feel your way around the situation to determine the best price for your product or service. And typically, companies are so focused on the product that they'll develop it and release it to the market only to find out it's not selling. Perhaps it's too expensive. But maybe, it's price is so low ("To gain market share.") that it is viewed as too cheap, such that prospective customers question its quality.

None of these approaches will maximize your revenue. In fact, without performing the right pricing process before you even start developing your product or service, you may well be spending time and money you don't need to. Worse, your released product may cause you more cash-flow problems than it solves.

Before the process is outlined, there are some examples to share:

[1] Initial price too low: By "talking with" several prospective customers, a client of mine had determined that the selling price needed to be $295 per year, for a recurring-fee product (*like* Turbo-Tax, only not). After several informal discussions over about three or four months, my client (while continuing to "talk with" prospects), raised his price to $695 per year, without serious pushback. Right before launch, I was able to help them implement the process described above. The "sweet spot" was $1,495 per year. 115% over the last "good" price, and over 400% more than his starting price. There were a couple customers who would have paid $20,000 per year. But that would have limited my client's market to about 2%.

And some prospects considered anything under $1,000 as too cheap, such that they would not buy it. This means that my client would have sold fewer products, at a lower price had he stuck with his gut, and those of a few vocal prospects. Bottom line: He asked the wrong question: "What would you pay?" yields too-low a price. Every time.

[2] Licensing fee too low: Another client had developed a product and was talking with one of the twelve OEM house in the world - to license their product. No production was required on the part of my client. Only developing a licensing contract, then watching the money roll in. The discussions between my client one the one OEM producer had the price settling on $8 per unit that the OEM house produced & sold. The OEM doubled the licensing fee to their end user, and planned on selling the option represented by my client's product.

I helped my client perform the pricing research - with the end-user. Not the OEM company. We found that the pricing sweet spot was $25, at list. This means that my client's customer was going to leave $9 on the table. When presented with that information, my client negotiated an agreement with the OEM for a $12 licensing fee. My client's effective net profit increased 50%, from $8 to $12. And, his customer also won. Subsequently, my client received an order for $250,000 worth of product licenses the first year. The additional revenue (and effectively their additional profit) was $83,333. The ROI on that pricing activity was over 10 to 1. And that is just for the *first* year.

[3] Price too high: A client had developed an idea, and asked that I join them in an interim executive role as CEO. The first order of business was to determine if there was a "there", there. That is, what would the market bear, and could we afford to launch into this market? Investment capital would be required, so we would need to make a case that we did our homework, and *knew* we could build a company.

The system was fairly complex, and had hardware, software and sensors to be developed. Through "manufacturing engineering", we determined that an installed solution that could save customers up to $200,000 a year would cost about $50,000, which meant we needed to sell it for about $70,000 to build a profitable, growing company.

When we performed the pricing research, we uncovered the true value prospective customers would place on it. Although one customer said he would pay more then $200,000 for our solution, the sweet spot for pricing was $6,500. Clearly, the market didn't value it, even though it would save serious money. Instead of sticking with an eventually-losing enterprise, we folded operations. It would have been unethical and immoral to try to raise any capital knowing this. And it would have been a terribly frustrating process - to try to sell to 5% of the market, and only (try to) build a $10 million a year company instead of the $100 - $200 million a year company we thought we could.

[4] Product re-defined: Another client of mine had developed a product with 18 features. The short version of this story is that - through pricing research - we found that 6 of those features were not valued at all, while an additional 3 features would *double the price*. (We performed pricing research with the 18-feature product, then updated the description, deleting reference to the 6 low-requirement features while adding the 3 most-mentioned features.)

Through this process, my client learned that he should have performed the pricing research before he ever wrote one line of code. He would have then concentrated on the most-wanted 15 features. He would have save himself time and money, and would have had a product worth twice as much.

There are plenty of other examples, most of which point to the fact that people tend to undervalue their products. Or worse, miss out on a unique opportunity to learn what else the market would value even more. Before developing the product or service.

The process described below is designed to help you determine your product's *value from your prospective customers'* perspective *before* you even start your design.

1) First, determine your product's features, functions and performance. Figure out what *you* think its benefits would be for customers. Then write up a *brief* description of this product.

2) With your product description in hand, choose five to ten potential customers in your market. With each of them, explain that you are doing market research and will need no more than four or five minutes of their time (and keep it to that.). After reading the product description ask them these five questions, *in this order*: [1] At what price would you consider this product expensive? [2] At what price would you consider this product *in*expensive? [3] At what price would you consider this product *too* expensive, such that you would not buy it? [4] At what price would you consider this product too cheap, so that you would question its quality? [5] What features would you add to increase the product's value to you?

3) Now, plot out the data points from the four pricing questions in Step 3) so that the four curves have the largest gap at one end and converge at the other. Look at where the four lines cross. The graph should look something like the figure, below.

4) Now determine if the prices named by these potential customers are anywhere near the range you thought. If not, you have *lots* of work to do to determine your potential customers' needs. Then look at the answers to the fifth question to see if there are features you could add to your product to increase its value. Refine your product description to reflect this.

5) If you need to, repeat this several times. Each time refine the product description until the price points that customers mention are high enough to yield your target margins. If they are consistently lower, then rethink your entire product or service.

6) Once you are sure customers will pay what you feel the product is worth, formalize your market research and do Steps 2) and 3) with enough potential customers to "smooth out" the curves.

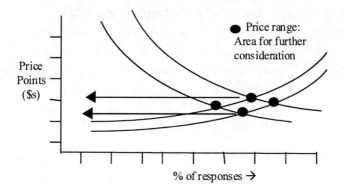

Congratulations. You have just defined how the market perceives the value of your product. You now have a clear roadmap on how to price your product and maximize your revenue.

Give it a try – you may be surprised by the results.

Maximize Marketing ROI: Tying Research to Sales

The most commonly stated desire of entrepreneurs is to increase revenue. But the direct and obvious paths to grow revenue do not always provide the best solutions, since what we think will work does not always work.

Case in point: Recently a software client wanted to improve sales performance. Although each individual sales person's annual performance was nowhere near the industry average, sales performance was not the real issue. The company, which recently started down a path of balancing their technical talent with a marketing team, was making great strides to improve their market presence and corporate image.

The "sales performance issue" actually rested on how well marketing and sales supported one another. Specific actions were taken to turbo charge sales. These included having marketing learn about their customers: how they buy, why they buy, what characteristics they feel are important about the products they purchase, and who they purchase them from. Marketing then used this information to integrate their efforts with sales, and balance corporate branding with a call to action. They changed from a one-sided marketing approach of increasing recognition of corporate brand – via trade-shows - to a more balanced approach, which included more direct-to-customers marketing efforts. This provided an action-oriented approach with outstanding results. An important outcome was not just the results obtained, but that the organization is learning the process to increase sales. More about actual results, later.

Implemented correctly, the following process can help you dramatically improve your marketing effectiveness and sales performance:

[1] Gather the facts: Many companies use gut feel as their guide. "Managing by fact" is a principle that can provide your team with essential information upon which to build marketing programs and propel your sales team's performance. Listen to prospects and customers. They can tell you all you really need to know in order to focus your marketing efforts and boost sales. What information do you need to get started?

> **External Research:** Provided below are just a few questions you should be asking:
>
> *How do customers buy?* Do they gather information through the web? By talking with sales people? From reading articles or case studies? By referrals from other customers or third party recommendations? From demonstrations? *Until you know how they gather their information, you do not know the best, most efficient ways to connect with them.*
>
> *Why do they buy?* What problems are they solving? How difficult are their efforts to build their solution once they purchase your product? *Until you know their specific reasons for purchasing, it is difficult to provide an offer that matches with their needs.*
>
> *What are their compelling reasons for selecting a particular product in your product category?* Is it price? Quality? Ease of

installation? Ease of use? Stature in their community for having purchased a particular solution? A specific feature or features? *Until you know their compelling reasons to buy, you cannot develop the right offerings for customers' needs.*

What are their compelling reasons for selecting a company or business partner)? Are they looking for the closest vendor to their company geographically? One who has been in business the longest? The most flexible payment terms? The easiest one to work with? The company best known in the industry? *Until you know what drives prospects to buy your offerings, you will not know how to best position your company. Correlating product branding with company branding is critical to offering the highest value for the price*

Internal Research: In addition to external research, it is important to uncover your selling patterns and determine your areas of weakness so you can change and improve.

Sales per person: Knowing the average sale per salesperson can help identify the sales situation. More importantly, it can help focus efforts in moving per sale averages up. A 25% increase per sale can add up quickly to a 25% improvement in the company's top line.

Close ratios: If closing leads garnered from trade shows generates a 2% close ratio, PR-related promotions generate 15%, and referrals generate 30%, then the marketing budget associated with generating sales should be balanced accordingly.

Available prospects and customers: If your prospect list is large and customer list is small, research into the prospects' needs can be very important. If your customer list is large, find out how you can dig deeper into their pockets by offering complementary products or by developing valuable product upgrades.

Assess your current marketing initiative mix: Products are promoted in many ways, including advertising, collateral promotional material, direct mail, event participation, guest editorials, case studies, Internet marketing, networking, newsletters, public relations, radio and TV, reference account development, seminars, sponsorships, telemarketing, telescreening, trade shows, and so on. Some companies like to focus their efforts in just a couple of these areas. This can lead to complacency and eventually lower sales. Unfortunately, customers' needs change over time, as do their buying habits. Assess your customers' needs frequently.

What is the return on investment for each marketing initiative? It is critically important to not only perform research, but also to perform test marketing programs, as well as measure their results. Only then will you really know how effective your marketing efforts are and what your next marketing and sales moves should be.

When you have gathered this information, you are on the path to [1] determining your return on investment for each marketing initiative, and [2] being able to re-direct your marketing efforts to crank up sales.

[2] Marketing initiatives: Based on external and internal market research, you can assess marketing initiatives before spending a great deal of money rolling out new programs. You will also be able to perform follow-up and measure the results. With this information, you will be in a position to dramatically improve sales.

Test: Once you learn the best ways to reach your potential customers, and how your competition does it, you can create marketing tests to check the effectiveness of what you think will work. No need to spend tens of thousands of dollars to find out a new promotion is going to fail. Spend a few hundred dollars. Try it out with at least 10 to 50 prospects. Provide a specific offer to buy your product, tied to the research you have performed.

Follow-up: A common mistake companies make is to send out hundreds of letters or postcards or create advertising or PR and then wait for the phone to ring. Especially in a business-to-business mode, you should know exactly who the right prospects are and how to best reach them. Involve your sales team during the marketing test, to ensure they know the marketing message and support it, and they know how to perform the follow-up.

Measure: Marketing initiatives need to be linked with actual sales. Learn how successful your efforts are by using simple statistics to keep track of whom you targeted and how they responded. Learn and then improve and then test again, if needed.

Engage: Once you know an initiative works (look for at least a ten-to-one simple return on investment), then increase your test initiative with two to twenty times the number of people used in the original test. Continue measuring, learning and selling. Depending on your industry focus and market, you may want to perform twenty to forty tests during the year and roll out five to twelve initiatives per year.

[3] Focus: Focusing marketing resources in those areas that produce the highest close ratios will increase sales effectiveness. If revenue is not a problem and corporate branding is, then corporate branding efforts make sense. A balanced marketing effort will support both sales and branding. But if sales are not expanding during an economic expansion, then marketing efforts need to focus on building revenue instead positioning the company.

[4] Learn & improve: The bad news in all this is that buying patterns shift all the time. Just when you think you have broken the code and are getting over a ten to one return on investment, customers change the way they buy. In good times and bad, continue researching and testing your marketing initiatives.

Recall the case that was discussed at the beginning of this chapter? The changes that were implemented resulted in an 80-to-1 improvement in their sales' effectiveness. That is, their return on investment increased eighty times.

Bottom Line: There is a sure way to improve revenue: listen to customers and prospects, test market to their stated needs, roll out marketing only after you have proven the initiative will work, focus your efforts based on what does work, and continuously learn. To do otherwise is like trying to hit a loud, quick-moving target in the dark with your eyes and ears covered.

Strategic Selling Skills for Technical Entrepreneurs

In today's high-speed, high technology business environment, many great new companies are built on ideas from technical people. This brings both good and bad news. Engineering creativity is the basis for American innovation and has brought the U.S. to world economic leadership. However, many outstanding ideas never get to market or receive funding. Or if they do, they often end in failure. Why? A common answer is that no one in the company really understands or *appreciates* effective sales techniques.

There are fundamental changes that technically minded entrepreneurs can make to propel their company to its next level. Ensuring that your company sells effectively is one of them. This chapter discusses just one channel – direct sales.

The Entrepreneur as Salesperson

"I'm the entrepreneur, not a salesperson." you might say. Not so. CEOs are the company's *ultimate* salesperson. CEOs need to *have* and *share* their vision with several stakeholders: customers, managers, employees, their banker, lawyers, VCs, potential acquirers, the press and others. They have to compel others to perform to their highest abilities, even when times are tough. And they have to sell prospective executives on why their company is the best place to continue that person's career. However, selling is the part of business most technology entrepreneurs least appreciate. Selling is not well understood, and is often not given proper support.

Critical Questions to Consider

Selling can be thought of as an exploration of needs and value. If there is high need for your company's products, their value will be much higher if the strategic need or the value proposition is clear. How do we better understand need and value? By asking questions and finding answers. Those answers will lead your company to increased sales and greater revenue.

- ✓ **What are you selling?** Typically, the great idea, codified in the latest product offering, is thought to be the thing that is being sold. In reality, the thing that is being bought is the *value* your product brings to customers, *not* the product itself. This fundamental concept is one that escapes many technology entrepreneurs. Yet it is the most profound question to be answered.

- ✓ **Why should customers be interested?** Understanding buying motivation requires discerning customers' problems. And in order to position your product as the premier solution to customers' needs, those needs require deep understanding. Which leads to…

- ✓ **What is the value proposition?** Once you clearly define customers' needs, you will be well on your way to defining the *value* of your solution. The higher the value, the more competitive your offering, the more you can charge, the higher your margins, the more valuable your company, the more wealth you create.

- ✓ **How do customers buy?** Understanding *how* customers buy (one to one) is critical to successfully marketing (one to many) your innovative solutions. Prior chapters have dealt with customer and market research. Suffice it to say, unless your company has thoroughly researched and understands *how* your customers buy, your salespeople cannot be effective in their jobs, no matter how good they are.

Motivating Salespeople

"How can I motivate our salespeople to higher performance?" This is a very important question technically trained entrepreneurs forget to ask. People become motivated to work harder when certain needs are met. Consider if your company is meeting these needs for your salespeople:

✓ **Goals:** Sales performance quotas and personal behavior goals should not be confused. Goals should be "SMART": Specific, Measurable, Attainable, Realistic, and Time-constrained." Of course, you will want consistent revenue, but defining and then encouraging specific *behavior* will ultimately morph your salespeople into a high-performance team. Examples are provided in the section on *Compensation* below. *Your most important task is learning what each sales person wants personally and then helping him or her achieve it.* This leadership secret is well understood by sales managers and can be applied by the small company CEO with great effect.

✓ **Performance Measurement:** Once goals have been agreed upon, it is important to regularly measure progress. This will help instill responsibility in sales people, as well as support corrective actions earlier rather than later. In this way, the sales process can be reviewed as well as individual performance.

✓ **Compensation:** A well-constructed commission structure can greatly enhance your long-term sales productivity. It takes time to develop, implement, and see results from a solid compensation plan. There are some critical elements to think about: Does the plan motivate continuous personal and departmental improvement? Does it support corporate objectives? Does it allow growth within the company?

Obviously, the plan needs to take into account the average selling price of products, the specific market, buying habits, etc. However, the plan should be responsive to and support the sales process. Additionally, there are a couple critical elements to consider in the plan: revenue objectives and personal behavior.

Examples of ways to motivate behavior to increase revenue include rewarding individual monthly performance, the meeting of individual and team-oriented objectives, and the development of new opportunities with existing customers; increasing the number of new customers, close ratios, and average revenue per sale; and perhaps even imposing a negative kicker for returns. These metrics can only be implemented if the company can actually track monthly performance in these areas. If your company cannot, you will need to reassess your internal accounting systems. Also, depending on your customer profile, consider a commission schedule that supports growing your salespeople into territory managers. In this way, you will be offering your salespeople advancement, and keeping talented people in your organization, instead of thinking about firing your most highly paid salespeople due to their large commission checks.

✓ **Excitement:** No one will readily admit they want "rah-rah" types of encouragement. However, if you can show genuine interest in their wins, and support them in their losses, your team will rise to even higher performance. Rewarding accomplishments can go a long way. For example, when your sales team brings in a tough or large client, reward them with a nice lunch, event ticket, or make a company announcement. This is especially powerful when coupled with consistent leadership.

✓ **Support:** To boost sales, the entire organization needs to work together. This is especially true of how marketing supports sales' efforts. To support direct sales' efforts, marketing initiatives need to balance corporate and product positioning with clear calls to action. Also, it can be tough to write big commission checks to salespeople, especially if you do not respect the sales function. However, salespeople should be in the position to make more than most senior managers if they are performing beyond expectations.

✓ **Consistency:** Changing the commission schedule every couple of months will rattle your sales team's confidence. If you can have aggressive, yet achievable sales goals, and consistently support the team in achieving these goals, your salespeople will believe you really care, and they will reward you with very hard effort and great results. Your trust in them will build their trust in you.

✓ **Respect:** It is very difficult for technology-minded entrepreneurs to appreciate salespeople. Because of their background and training, technology entrepreneurs tend to view salespeople as a necessary evil instead of a critical element to the success of the company. Engineers look for facts to solve difficult problems, and salespeople have to be incredibly flexible in order to make the sale. These two personality types do not mix well, unless both sides recognize and respect the value each brings to the organization. Just as every person needs a heart and brain, every high-tech organization needs engineering *and* sales.

Bottom line: Without sales, you have no business. And if the CEO does not respect the sales function, the key points made above will not help you.

More Questions to Explore

How can we improve our sales *process*? There are several ways to create and successfully implement an appropriate sales process, including using new management tools for process development and codification, integrating your marketing and sales processes, integrating sales with your organizational development, and testing and measuring the results of your process to know where it can be improved. The specifics are beyond the scope of this chapter.

What should our sales organization look like? Your sales organization is a function of your products' average selling prices, channel mix, product complexity and myriad other factors. The specifics for organizational aspects are also beyond the scope of this chapter, but should be considered when analyzing your sales capabilities.

The Bottom Line

The sooner you can agree that sales is as important as technology to your company's growth; and can accurately assess customers' needs, sales employees' personal goals, and your products' value proposition; the sooner you can improve your top-line revenue. Quickly coming to grips with the issues outlined here can be extremely valuable to your company. Especially since time really is worth more than money.

How to Attract Significantly More Customers

How to turbo-charge your marketing & sales efforts
Do you have all the customers you need? Are you looking for
cost-effective ways to attract more customers? Have you tried
advertisements, newsletters, trade-shows, brochures, social
media / SEO efforts, and dozens of other ways - without the
success you would like? Are you happy with the status-quo?
Would you like to turbo-charge your sales efforts, maybe double
or triple your sales, without paying a fortune?

There are several marketing secrets that no one really discusses.
In fact, if you talk with a hundred different marketing
consultants, you are likely to get 99 different opinions about
what to do. And, probably in their own areas of expertise. You
can't afford to try them all, but isn't that what you've been
doing? Without the success you would like?

If you are ready to learn changes you can make in order to boost
revenue and your company's value, then read on.

What does "strategic marketing" mean?
The secret to increasing sales has everything to do with being
effective, instead of efficient. And it has everything to do with
"managing by facts," instead of through seat-of-the-pants
marketing. If one marketing method brings ten times the
response rates over a second method, then why even spend a
dime on that second way? Yet time after time, that is exactly
what business owners do. Because that's what they think
"marketing" is: doing lots of "marketing". This approach is
quite natural and pervasive, but it can be very ineffective. If you
are interested in making your trade shows the best they can be,

but they yield the lowest close ratios, then why make it perfect? Or do it at all? Find out what works and do that, instead.

The difference between tactical marketing and strategic marketing is simple: Tactical marketing is "doing stuff," and strategic marketing is focused on getting results. It has to do with knowing, instead of guessing (through marketing failures), what will and won't work ... before you spend loads of cash on any particular marketing initiative.

Doing six marketing "things"... may generate a lot of leads... but if they are not the right leads, nor converting to sales - in the shortest time, what do you do? You add a seventh "thing." This spreads out your limited marketing $s even thinner. If you knew which one marketing approach gave you the largest return on your investment, wouldn't you simply do just that one thing? Why do more? Spend more? Get lower returns? This just doesn't make sense, yet business owners do it all the time... because most "marketing types" are great at marketing tactics - not necessarily marketing strategies. In tactical marketing, more (spending) is better. In strategic marketing less (spending) is better. And just talking about strategic marketing doesn't mean you're actually doing it.

The key notion here is... how can you leverage your limited marketing resources to yield even greater returns?

Are you ready to turbo-charge your sales? How would you like to:

- Learn how to attract more customers, by spending *less* on marketing?
- Have your customers spend more on your products and services?
- Double or triple your sales' effectiveness?

The marketing secret discussed in this article requires that you are 100% open to change and learning, that you stop making even the smallest assumptions about your marketplace, and that you may need to learn a new language... your customers'.

What can you do to attract more customers?

Determine exactly what you need to know in order to attract more of your "A" customers. Not the "market research" that tells you how many competitors you have, and what other product / service choices your customers have. Nor is this about "the sale:" where you are having a one to one conversation, finding out specific needs. This secret will help you communicate with your prospects in the way that they want to buy… from you.

The four things you need to know about your customers and prospects are:

- Who are they?
- What are they buying?
- Why are they buying?
- How are they making their purchasing decisions?

The specific answers to these general questions will [1] show the way to bring in business, [2] help you go after those customers who will provide you the biggest bang for the buck, [3] enable you to develop exactly what you say to prospects, and [4] approach them how they want to be approached.

Who are your customers?

Specifically, given a choice between customers who spend an average of $1,000 on your company's offerings and those who spend $5,000, wouldn't you rather find those who spend five times as much? You can also assess their sales cycle, lifetime value, gross margins, etc. Determining exactly and statistically who your preferred customers are - and what attributes and characteristics they have - will allow you to spend time only on the best prospects. What is it about your best customers that make them spend more? If you don't know, wouldn't it make sense to find out? Once you do, you have started figuring out how to address a "5X" challenge. That is, if you solve this one problem, you may have an opportunity to increase your sales by a factor of five. And since you are going after 5X buyers, your cost-to-acquire decreases, enabling you to focus better, and potentially spend even less time and money on marketing.

What are they buying?
Specifically, what benefits and features are they buying? What tangible attributes do they want? Are they buying your products and services because they are faster? Smaller? More durable? Integrated? Easily changed? By answering this question, you will be able to learn which of your offerings' features to discuss with prospects. If there are 25 features, and your prospects are only interested in five, then why spend any time discussing the other twenty? This is where you start learning their exact language. Sometimes a one word change in your message can make a significant difference.

Why are they buying?
Specifically, what are your prospects' underlying motivations for purchasing your products/services? If you can uncover their reasons for buying from you, you will be able to address these reasons when you market and sell to them. Your task is to find their intangible rationale for their buying patterns. And do so statistically.

How are they buying?
If everyone in your business-to-business industry is presenting at trade shows, but your customers buy because of referrals, why go to trade shows? If coupons overwhelmingly bring them to your retail store, why advertise in the yellow pages? The methods you like to use may have worked in the past, but times change. And they're changing rapidly. A much more effective way is to learn before you spend money on low-return methods. And the best way to do that is to statistically learn your customers' preferred methods.

I use the terms "specific" and "statistically" for each of these four areas. The reason is to avoid the "loudest, last customer" syndrome. You know… that one customer or prospect who was/is insistent that you do this or that… while nine out of ten others quietly prefer something else. If you don't uncover the hidden majority-driven preferences, you will be forever lagging in sales.

Why do we answer the four questions above? We want to learn what we need to do to attract more customers. Specifically, we want to better understand the following areas:

- Markets: Only after we better learn who are our best customers, can we more effectively target them. We can reduce spending in areas that attract the wrong customers, and improve our return on investment.
- Messages: Only after we understand what our customers' are buying and why they are buying, we will be able to develop specific messages that map into their mind… that resonate with their thinking and feeling.
- Methods: Only after we determine how our customers make their purchase decisions will we be able to use the appropriate methods for the appropriate market, in the way they buy.

If each of the answers to the four questions (who, what, why, how) yields a 3X to 5X improvement in performance, then combining the results can yield significant corporate performance improvements. You might be able to focus on only one customer type, with fewer products - the exact opposite of our natural instincts - which is to create more products, go into adjacent markets and try to "buy" market share. These typically fail - unless you are made of cash and can afford many failures. Most clients I work with don't have the luxury of extra time and money and want great results sooner, not later.

What results can you achieve?

Every company, industry, and market is different. However, here are typical results our clients have achieved as a result of using this secret, in conjunction with six others:

- Doubled the number of customers in three months.
- Increased available cash in the bank from $150K to $1.4 million in 18 months.
- Raised prices 50% and increased sales as a result.
- Increased revenue 71% in three months, doubling within one year.
- Obtained direct marketing response rate of 25% from prospects & 40% from customers.
- Increased company value from prior offers of $1 million - to $20 million in six months.
- Grossed an additional $500,000 in three months ($233K/month average, before).

What to do tomorrow - to start attracting new customers.

At the end of in-house seminars I present to CEOs, participants ask me how to get started right away.

- First, perform an internal assessment of your customers. Analyze your customer database (you *do* have a database of customers, right?). There are several analyses you can perform, but sort on total revenue per customer, gross margin, sales cycle, life-of-customer value, costs to acquire, etc.
- Second, figure out who your top (i.e preferred) customers are - their characteristics and attributes.
- Third, develop and deploy a survey that contains both open-ended and closed-ended questions to determine the nuances your seat-of-the-pants approach can't.
- Fourth, analyze, then synthesize the results to statistically get at the information that you need in order to develop highly-effective marketing.
- Fifth, test (market, message, method) what you have learned to validate you are no longer making assumptions.

When rolling out your new fact-based marketing initiative, there are some great marketing, advertising, PR and "marcom" firms who can help you achieve success. You will be able to choose them with great confidence that you now know the right markets, messages, and methods. You will no longer be making any assumptions. And you can be assured your marketing will be significantly more effective.

If you don't know how - or don't have time to make this happen, hire someone who has done this many times before. Isn't your company worth it?

A final thought
If this were easy, then everyone would be doing it. It is the hard work that pays dividends - not only in the long run - it can also dramatically increase your business in very short order. It is far easier to simply "do marketing" than it is to know which is the right marketing to do. So step back, think, plan and go attract more customers.

Note: This chapter is the basis for my second book: "How to Attract Significantly More Customers... in good times and bad" – available directly from www.synergy-usa.com's, or through Amazon.

Section 4

Improving Operational Performance

- **Organizing for the Customer**
- **Achieving Peak Company Performance**
- **How to Hire the Best People**
- **How to Predict the Future**
- **How to Manage Projects**
- **How to Define Products**
- **Solutions for the New Millennium**
- **Reasons Why Some Organizations Perform Poorly**

The purpose of this section is to take a closer look at what differentiates high-performance organizations from others. Every entrepreneur is tasked with integrating their area of expertise with others within the company, so that true synergies can exist throughout the entire company. Just as we need a heart and a brain to survive and thrive, so do organizations require market-driven (flexible) groups to find and define new markets and technical departments to innovatively develop new products and services to address these new market opportunities. Techniques on strategic planning, organizational development, hiring processes, and product definition are discussed – to share new ways to turbo-charge your company.

Organizing for the Customer

Ever wonder how you can get your products and services to market faster than your competition, with features and performance so advanced your customers don't mind paying more for *your* solution? So do a lot of chief executives.

Think about what affects your company: customers' ever changing needs, competition's rapid cycle time, technology's dizzying pace, etc. Yet, if you take a moment to think about your real span of control, you will see that it involves none of these external factors. The things you can actually *do* something about are limited to those who are reporting to you, your leadership and management style, and operational success factors. These are the important aspects of your business that *you* can control and – with the right decisions – can dramatically change the performance of your company. An extremely important success factor is how you are organized.

How often have you heard of these situations:
[1] A marketing Account Executive (AE) gets a call from a customer who needs a solution to a problem. The AE gets excited because he feels a new requirement has been stated that "Only my company can develop." which might even be true. He goes to an engineer to discuss the need. The engineer gets really excited because this new need has never been addressed. It will challenge the engineer in ways she's never been challenged before. The AE calls back the customer and

promises a solution is going to be developed, and even gives a price and time frame.

[2] Taking a new class, an engineer has just figured out how to solve a problem she's been trying to solve for a very long time. She takes it to the department manager and weaves a tale of technical ecstasy, if only a customer can be found. The manager recognizes the value of the solution and authorizes another engineer to support the first in converting the idea into a high-level concept test model to see if there might be a customer for it.

The Missing Ingredient:
In both these cases, whether the company employs five people or 500, only two perspectives have been addressed: that of one customer and that of a technical person. These business questions were never asked:

➢ Is developing this idea in our company's charter?
➢ If this is a huge opportunity, what is the revenue potential?
➢ Is this something we really want to do?
➢ Is this something we *should* be doing?
➢ Do we have the capability?
➢ Does this idea correspond with our vision and mission?
➢ Is our corporate vision so broad it prevents the kind of focus we need?
➢ If the idea is covered by the mission statement, do we have the core competencies to do the job? If not, do we need more people or money? Can we find what we need outside?
➢ Do we need to develop or buy new core technology?
➢ What is the relative priority of this project with respect to others we are doing or considering?
➢ Is the idea do-able? Will it be profitable? Can we pull it off, and everything else, too?

Detailed answers are not required at an initial level, but these questions *must* be asked, if only in a cursory way.

Marketing's role is to bring the customers' perspective to the company (voice of the customer). Engineering's role is to ensure technical capability can be applied to problems to create value-adding solutions to customers' problems (voice of technology). Given a choice between erring on the side of the customer or addressing the business issues, Marketing will tend to make decisions in favor of the customer, even at the expense of revenue and profits. This is what Marketing is being paid to do. Given a choice between erring on the side of being technically correct or addressing the business issues, Engineering will tend to make decisions in favor of what is technically correct, even at the expense of revenue and profits. This is what Engineering is being paid to do.

In an organization without a functional leader who pays attention to the voice of business, corporate issues will always be subservient to Engineering and Marketing.

A Balanced Approach is Needed:
Many companies feel that their marketing, sales and engineering departments are able to address *all* the day-to-day, as well as strategic issues, facing the company. What is typically missing in this arrangement is a group or department that is chartered to deal with *business issues*. Most organizations believe they address their business issues with senior management's attention, or by having project managers reporting to Engineering, or product managers reporting to Marketing. The problem is that when critical trade-offs need to be made, as they always do, *whomever the*

product or project manager reports to yields the deciding perspective. A generalized matrix will help make this clear:

Department making decision: Who "wins" or "loses"...

Decisions required →:	Customer	Technical	Business
➢ Marketing	Win	Loss	Loss
➢ Engineering	Loss	Win	Loss

Clearly, not all decisions cause win-loss situations. In fact, the organizations that strive for multi-win solutions usually out-perform those who do not. Given critical real-time decisions that require discussion and different points of views, business concerns will tend to lose out over marketing and technical concerns, when there is no "voice of business" function, reporting to the president.

Giving business an equal voice in the decision making process provides balance and stability. It forces robust business discussions on an on-going basis, and causes all sides of the story to be told. Additionally, when business concerns are implemented correctly, conflicts between and among projects can be worked out at lower levels, *freeing up senior management to concentrate on more strategic issues.*

The best functional representation of the Voice of Business is project / program management. A strategic PM role, reporting to the CEO, is typically missing in technology companies. Tactical "gofers" are usually used, and the voice of business cannot be led from this level.

Pushing Decisions to Lower Levels to Achieve Greater Performance:

Since business decisions happen in real-time, the President or Chief Executive Officer (and certainly the Chairman) cannot possibly make *all* the business decisions. These need to be made at the lowest *possible* levels within the organization.

Addressing the three major areas of greatest value to an effective decision-making company, a hybrid organization (which balances functional responsibilities with project and product responsibilities) yields better decisions than purely functional organizations.

A company's *business* performance is only as good as the cumulative performance of all its projects and products, whether these are solution oriented, pure products, or pure service projects. For this reason, to radically improve *business* performance, it is imperative to radically improve *project* performance, across the board, on a *project by project* basis. Enhancing project performance requires decision-making improvements. Having a department chartered with the *business responsibility* of each and every project ensures that the company can be as responsive and proactive to customers and markets as possible.

Those who feel they will be adversely affected by such a change are usually the ones who are the most resistive to change (typically people in marketing and engineering). Given insufficient information about a change, people tend to provide some level of overt or covert resistance.

However, once they see how they are *positively* affected, their acceptance is assured. In the larger picture, their roles free up. They enjoy what they are doing more and become more effective, a real advantage to organizational improvement.

Implementing change is no easy matter

In the Harvard Business Review book *Critical Path to Corporate Renewal*[5], Beer, Eisenstat and Spector state that organizational changes which are forced from the top *tend* to fail while changes which are implemented as solutions to specific and obvious problems *tend* to succeed. Certainly these two approaches do not guarantee success or failure; but increased tendencies toward success – if the plan is directed at a specific problem – are decidedly there.

With this in mind, any changes to the way a company operates must focus on *specific* solutions to current and future challenges. Although financial support for improved business performance through change must come from senior management, the specific approaches must come from those who can make the change successful.

Addressing Organizational Issues of Change

There are several issues, which must be considered prior to and during any transition to improve an organization. In order to successfully affect organizational and process changes, the following questions need answering:

➤ How will a firm senior management commitment be obtained?

➤ How will mid-level and lower-level management and project personnel be encouraged to buy into a product development process?

➤ What will be the first project to be managed, and how will it be implemented?

➤ Are existing projects affected? If so, how and when?

➤ How will the processes be communicated to employees and how will they be trained?

➤ What tools and reporting methods will be used?

Successful companies understand the need to bring the business function on par with marketing and engineering functions to ensure a *balanced* approach is used to develop and implement corporate strategies to meet objectives. To be successful, this third function must have the proper authorities and responsibilities to ensure the *business perspective* is adequately addressed. These improvements will ensure resources are applied in a focused manner, which yields better products faster and more targeted to your customers' needs.

Bringing it All Together
To increase success, it is imperative that leaders *recognize the value that a balanced approach brings to your company.*

By balancing the voices of the customer, technology and business within your organizational structure, better decisions will be made at lower levels, freeing you up to do what you have to and enjoy doing: thinking about the future of your company. Your company will be even better aligned with the customer since the more integrated organizations are, the better they perform; and the more focused they are on customers' needs instead of cross-functional conflicts, the higher the revenue and profit.

Achieving Peak Company Performance

Many times entrepreneurs ask -"How can I turbo-charge my organization?" Of course, this usually means, "How can I increase revenue without spending more money?" Let's review a few ways your organization can achieve superior performance:

✓ **Focus**: With limited resources, companies need to choose their battles carefully. All too often leaders authorize a project because they can. Successful companies focus on their core competencies and align them with their customers' needs. Develop a strategy to encourage calculated risk-taking, *within the focus you define*.

There are many reasons for a company to lose focus. If the founder/president is technically oriented, s/he will tend to want to create products for every idea they have. If the founder/president has a marketing background, s/he all too often wants to address *every* customer need. Since no company has infinite resources, both approaches present a potential for disaster. Therefore, companies must choose only what they can realistically afford to do and no more. Otherwise, *all* projects will suffer.

One very entrepreneurial client was successfully selling only one type of product in ten years. They were working on 38 more projects, yet none were close to being completed.

After working with them, a process was implemented to evaluate opportunities relative to predetermined strategic and financial performance criteria. Consequently, they cut the number of projects in half. In addition, processes for improving existing products and developing new products were established.

The results? Within eighteen months they had introduced six new products, with three more in line for completion in the next six months. Revenue increased from under $3 million to over $5 million and available, sales-generated cash grew by nearly ten times, to almost a million and a half dollars.

Some questions to ask yourself regarding focus were identified in the previous section. If you are truly honest with yourself, the answers may surprise you. They may even help you make those tough decisions every leader *must* make to accomplish high level goals. The very act of asking these questions of yourself and your employees shows that there *is* a process, resulting in employee buy-in. And buy-in is essential for motivating people to perform beyond their norm.

On the quantitative side, can your company identify its assumptions about a project? What is the expected return on investment (ROI)? Why spend money on a project whose ROI lingers at the low end of expectations? Will the project position the company for the future and help it leapfrog the competition, arriving at a more reasonable ROI downstream?

These are just the top-level questions. You can develop your own set of questions to help you focus your company's efforts on those projects that provide the highest return.

✓ **Reward the right behavior**: Many company leaders actually reward bad behavior because the employee or manager "was being entrepreneurial and taking risks", even though those risks were detrimental to the rest of the organization. To avoid this problem, you must clearly define your company and unambiguously communicate your expectations.

However, risk taking is essential for success. That is the good news. The bad news is that unfocused and unmanaged entrepreneurialism will invariably misuse scarce resources. This organizationally immature behavior will drive the company out of business if it is not balanced with sufficient leadership and management experience. People usually do not want to be controlled, so they resist planned processes. However, high creativity within a controlled process-oriented framework can yield a work environment that is conducive to phenomenal team-centered problem solving, and consequently lead the company to accomplish much more with fewer resources.

✓ **Encourage small wins**: This is Project Management 101A. Everyone feels good when milestones are reached. It is also one of the most over-looked, simple to use methods available. Understanding customers' needs and then taking the time to plan the project in sufficient detail to uncover small wins will also uncover risks and allow the project team to tackle huge problems in a manageable way. Coupling this concept with a "requirements flow" process will yield excellent results. Encouraging small wins creates a positive team psyche, since positive feelings are contagious and build upon themselves. Small wins also encourage top level *goals* to become the project team's *commitments*.

✓ **Stop changing everything**: Some presidents lose the respect of their managers and employees because the leader uses a "Book of the Month" management style. This demoralizes and de-motivates employees, and drags down company performance. Employees can see right through this lack of professional experience.

Providing a stable environment will put your employees at ease and allow them to concentrate on helping you achieve your corporate goals and objectives.

✓ **Change everything**: Contrary to the previous point, it is also essential to make sure you address challenges and opportunities as they arise. Change is everywhere, and in fact, at a deep level your employees want change when it is obvious the change will make their lives easier. So be open about accepting ideas from your employees, vendors, customers and other partners. A great idea that addresses a specific issue and can be implemented with the full buy-in of those employees most affected can reap huge rewards. Just be aware that people resist top-down directives. Have a great reason to make the change and then listen. Take time to plan the change and inform and involve those who will be affected. Allow them time to buy into the process by having their voices heard. The first Golden Rule of business may be "Those who have the gold make the rules." But the second Golden Rule surely is: "Those who *do* the work need to *plan* the work." This goes for projects as well as company change efforts.

✓ **Communication**: Improving communication cannot be emphasized enough. It is imperative that an organization implement processes to deal with the vast amount of information and the geometrically increasing change that exists as the organization grows.

It is becoming clear that technology is getting ahead of our ability to manage it. It is therefore imperative to have systems, methods and processes established to effectively and efficiently communicate among and between organizations. From the customers' requirements to product strategies, to product design criteria, to product testing procedures – all aspects of the business must have clear and consistent communication protocols.

The best way to address this challenge is to first understand it exists. Then recognize the need to tackle the largest information bottlenecks first. Adding expensive computer networking systems will not solve the problem. Computer networks only speed up whatever communication methods already exist. It is critical to understand best-in-class processes to speed inter-organizational communication and work towards developing and implementing the right methods for *your* organization. (And yes, a consultant can help.) Communication is so important you should be staying up at night, thinking about how your competitor is probably doing something about it right now.

✓ **Efficiency vs. effectiveness**: Balance your tactical efforts (efficiency) with your strategic efforts (effectiveness). By focusing on your customers' needs and then systematizing these efforts via codified processes, company performance will soar. Many new processes implemented by organizations appear to bog everything down. Which is why so many people resist implementing them. However, if you understand that *how* things get done is critical to leveraging your limited resources to accomplish more than you ever thought possible, you will begin to see that doing the wrong thing very well is far worse than doing the right thing poorly.

Small and large companies can benefit by assessing their strategic and tactical processes to see if they are in synch. Are corporate objectives being hindered due to operational or project teams not being on board with the corporate vision? Is the strategic planning process overwhelmed by day-to-day panics caused by a lack of strategic planning?

It is essential that *what* the company focuses on needs to be balanced with *how* the company does its work. The question is: How do you balance these typically diametrically opposed situations? Simple: Integrate the Shewhart Cycle of "Plan, Do, Check, and Act[5]".

✓ **Requirements**: Customers change their minds. Markets shift. Competitors develop new products and new technologies that make planning seem like a waste of time. "How can we be flexible if we take time to plan?" you might ask.

Best-in-class companies understand the need to clearly define customers' needs, have processes in place to obtain and communicate these needs throughout the organization, and flow these needs into the high-level system's requirements. From these requirements come top level design requirements, then detailed design specifications, and then integration and testing requirements. Coupling a requirements flow-down process with improvements in cross-functional communication, and then linking tactics to strategies, drives higher-performing organizations. This involves planning at both the strategic and tactical levels.

The common theme to achieving peak company performance is focus. By focusing on the *right* projects, encouraging small wins, and communicating and rewarding professional team-oriented behavior, your company's performance will take off.

How to Hire the Best People

Have you ever had to let someone go because they didn't live up to your expectations? Or they turned out to be completely different from what their resume indicated? Or you got exactly what you wanted but not what you needed? If these scenarios sound familiar, then you are not alone. Especially when it comes to executive recruiting. In fact, many recruitment efforts end in failure for some very fundamental reasons:

- No process.
- Hire on skills / fire on traits.

For instance, by defining a repeatable process, you will save yourself a lot of time and aggravation, minimize your legal exposure, and dramatically increase your hiring success rate.

We also tend to hire people based on skills, and then let them go on to their personality.

Once you develop your recruiting process, you will be able to learn where it fails you and modify it for future use. This way, you can achieve repeatable successes and minimize the time you spend on this important and time-consuming effort. You can also build in capabilities that will give you information about an applicant's personal traits.

Some things to consider, include:

Determine your general organizational roles, responsibilities and relationships: Through strategic planning you should have a good
idea of who you are and your company's needs and focus. This will go a long way in defining your organization, now and for the future.

Pamela Jones, Principal of **JONES AND JONES,** a technology search firm, told me, *"High-growth companies (start-up and well established) have special requirements. Their executive team needs to constructively embrace the personal and professional changes required to sustain ongoing corporate growth. This is essential for future success."*

Define your specific organizational needs: Once you have taken the time to develop your corporate strategic plan, organizational roles and operational objectives should be clear. These roles and objectives form the basis for defining the job.

Write a position description: For so many reasons, it is imperative to define your specific requirements. Without a written position description, you are setting yourself and your company up for failure. These requirements will form the basis for your resume screening criteria and interview questions. The position description should contain these elements: position title, who they report to, summary of the role, responsibilities and duties of the position, general and specific skills required, mandatory experience and education, and preferred experience and education.

Determine your recruitment budget: What can you afford? What can you *not* afford? If this position goes unfilled, what will be the result? How do your salaries fit with your budget?

Can you fill it with an "interim hire" – to buy you some time? Keep these consequences in mind as you plan.

Spread the word: Clearly, the first and best source of new employees is through current (high-performance) employees. In addition to placing advertisements, offer incentives to current employees to keep a sharp look-out for potential new employees, and network like crazy.

Iris Sasaki, owner of Iris Sasaki-HR, LLC recently told me *"An outstanding employee is the 'golden goose' of recruiting -- s/he delivers applicants prescreened and ready for the next step. So, reach in your pocket and pay that 'finder's fee', the ROI will amaze you."*

Put the full job description on your web site and drive candidates there. Monster.com (general position posting), craigslist.com and other web sites can be very effective, but before using them, decide if you can afford to pay relocation costs. Specialized postings (for example, www.execunet.com) target specific audiences and can be used to locate excellent candidates.

Network: Share your needs with your employees, business associates, and acquaintances in professional associations. They may know great candidates.

Measure Results: Use a special e-mail address for responses to the job, so you can track where leads come from and campaign effectiveness.

Pre-screen: Since you spent time developing your position description, you already have the basis for screening resumes. If the level of experience you seek is five years mandatory in that role, then four years' experience is insufficient. Period. If you do not stick to your specific requirements in screening, you may be liable for lawsuits, so be sure to define your requirements carefully.

Interview: With a well-written position description, you also have the basis to create your interview questions. Make sure they tie back to the requirements of the job. Ask questions that encourage the candidate to demonstrate how they will solve problems and overcome challenges at your company. Look for behavioral patterns to check how the candidate will fit in with your current employees. Organizational development consultant **Kathy Holmquist** says, "*In the long run, intangible competencies will make or break the person. These are the underlying characteristics of a person which enable them to deliver superior performance in their role.*"[7]

Reference checks: Due to potential legal issues, most reference checks seem to be useless. Ask the candidate's references if they would hire the person again, and why or why not. You can also ask for the names of people who know the candidate and interview them. This is a common practice when doing national security background checks.

Team interviews: Be sure the candidate's peers get a chance to interview, but pre-brief them on the legalities of interviewing. This includes not asking about age, marital status, religious affiliation, etc. Check for "fit". Determine if the candidate's style matches with those s/he will be working for and with. You want success this time around so you don't have to do it again in six months.

Their questions: What questions did the candidate ask? Was s/he interviewing you too? Did they ask about your goals and objectives? The specific goals for this position? The budget? If they do not know what you really want the successful candidate to do, how much they have to work with, and if they do not ask for a chance to meet the people that they will need to lead to make it all happen, then they do not know enough to take the job. If they do not ask these questions, they would rather leap before they look, and you should not want to hire them.

The negotiation: If the candidate is not right, then $1 a year is too much to pay them. If they are the right candidate and can help you achieve your corporate objectives, then you should consider a total compensation package that includes salary, a performance-based bonus (increasing this can lower the base pay), stock options (vested over time or performance based), and a reasonable benefits package that fits with your current benefits program.

Although this is a simplified description of the process, it covers quite a few issues you need to address when trying to hire the best. Skip any of these essential areas and you are sure to regret it later.

"The major reason searches fail is the lack of process," says **Frank Moscow**, President of **The Brentwood Group, Ltd**.[7] *"Successful companies recognize the value of having well thought out product development or manufacturing processes, but many organizations don't apply the same discipline to their hiring process. Just like world class manufacturing and product development processes, a strong strategic staffing process increases success metrics while reducing cycle time."*

When searching for that special hire, you are not alone.

Professional recruiters should be able to help you in this area. An in-depth graphic of the hiring process begins on the next pages.

Basic Process Flow for Hiring the Best

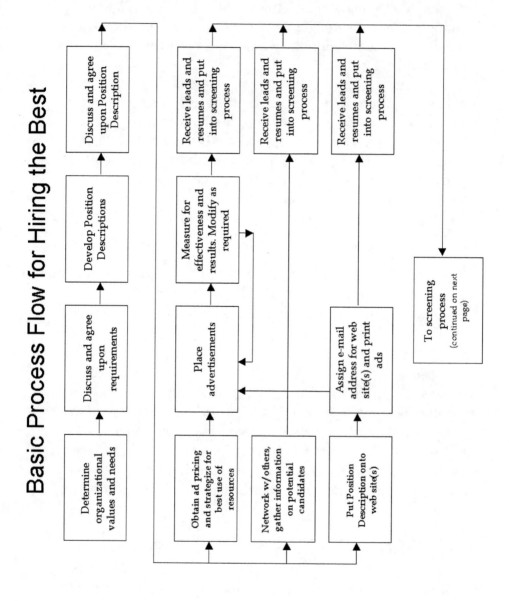

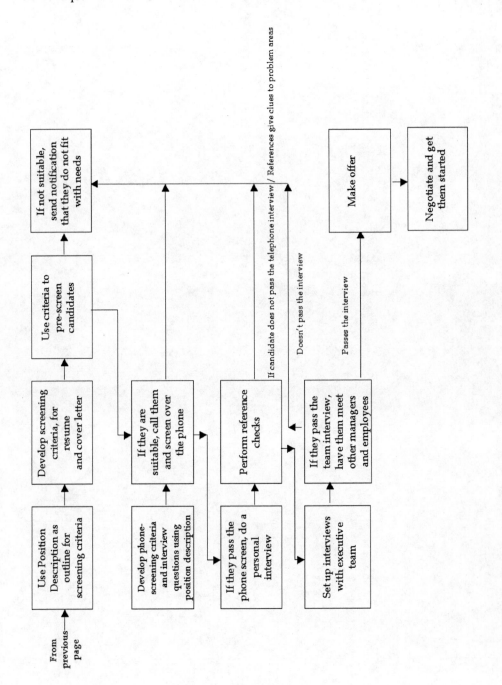

How to Predict the Future

Every entrepreneur would like to make the best decisions and know the resulting outcome ahead of time. Some make decisions based on facts, others use gut feel to guide their company's course. Decisions based on *excellent* information tend to be better, since "managing by fact" consistently provides higher quality decisions than any other method. However, *all* decisions are emotional decisions.

So how do we deal with this apparent paradox? Is it gut feel or logic? Which is better?

Clearly, the more information you have, the more dependable your gut feel will be. In order to make the best decisions, the question is, "How can I get the highest quality information in the least amount of time?" But before we look at just a few of the tools for making better decisions, we need to take a step back and review the way your company can provide the most value to your customers in a predictive manner. The most fundamental building blocks in exceptional decision making are data. Often thought of as "knowledge", data without analysis are useless. Data must be transformed into information and then knowledge for people and organizations to make great decisions.

If you think about the progression of many organizations' attempts to gain good information, things will become clearer. First there were *Data Processing Departments*. Then there were / are *"Management Information Systems"*. Now a

Chief Knowledge Officer is all the rage. Over the past 10 years this progression has been quite predictable. The more an organization moves through this *value sequence*, (see graphic on the next page) the better the decisions and the more agile the company.

There are several computer tools and business methods that can aid you and your company in creating the knowledge needed to help make exceptional decisions. This, in turn, will help you predict the future.

Crystal Ball: This software package, by Decisioneering[8] (which was acquired by Oracle), integrates seamlessly with Microsoft Excel to support your decisions, whether strategic or tactical in nature. It uses Monte Carlo simulations based on your assumptions and input. With this software, you and your staff can assess the likely outcome of any series of difficult and complex situations.

Earned Value: An excellent way to predict the future on a project-by-project basis, Earned Value provides an extremely powerful projection method, giving insights into current project variances and accurately *predicting* future project performance. This improves predictive capabilities to meet time-to-market, cost and performance requirements. (For a detailed write-up, email the author through www.synergy-usa.com.)

Sales Projections: You can predict the future without using these software programs. By (1) clarifying the total market size, (2) defining the critical assumptions in acquiring the customer's business, and (3) being realistic about your company's ability to capitalize on your marketing and sales initiatives, you can determine *optimistic, pessimistic,* and *most* *probable* sales and profit forecasts. Additionally, this method can be used to judge the value of potential products competing internally for limited resources, so that effective decisions can be made as to the value to your customers and your company's top line. Integrated with the pricing method shared in the section "How to Value-Price Your Products and Services," and the organization model discussed in "Organizing for the Customer," you could be well on your way to maximizing your sales and profits.

As variously attributed to Alan Kay (Xerox PARC luminary), Jason Kaufmann and Peter Drucker: "The best way to predict the future is to *create it*." With these tools an organization can iteratively ask itself, "What about doing things *this* way, or *that*?" and then modify its decisions based on the outcome of *simulated* plans, before spending time and money on wasted efforts.

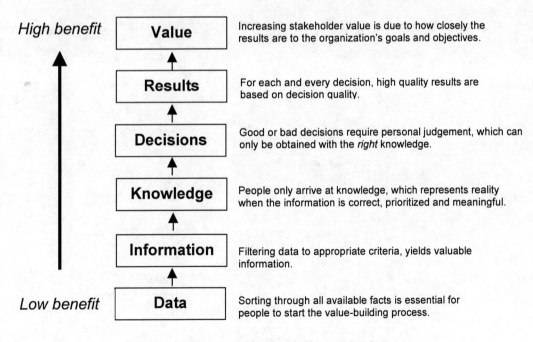

High benefit

Value — Increasing stakeholder value is due to how closely the results are to the organization's goals and objectives.

Results — For each and every decision, high quality results are based on decision quality.

Decisions — Good or bad decisions require personal judgement, which can only be obtained with the *right* knowledge.

Knowledge — People only arrive at knowledge, which represents reality when the information is correct, prioritized and meaningful.

Information — Filtering data to appropriate criteria, yields valuable information.

Low benefit

Data — Sorting through all available facts is essential for people to start the value-building process.

Diagram © Copyright 1991 Phoenix Management, Inc.

How to Manage Projects

Regardless of revenue, your company's profits depend upon controlling costs. This chapter deals with minimizing the expenses in developing new products and reducing the time it takes to get those products to market.

By addressing new product development in the way described here, your company will be better positioned to respond to the customers and beat your competitors to market. Although an "Agile" approach can help you speed products to market, these six critical points will help you bring products to market, more quickly:

Identify Key Project Phases

Opportunity Assessment and Qualification
This earliest phase begins with recognizing the customers' emerging needs, and ends with completing the evaluation of the opportunity. This assessment should include, but not be limited to, interaction with the customer, qualification of the business opportunity, and presentation of findings and results to senior management.

Pre-Planning
This phase begins with the decision to follow the opportunity, and ends with defining and documenting a preliminary winning solution to the customers' requirements. A "plan for a plan" is developed which defines the resources, and schedules, and requirements for planning the project.

This is to avoid random expenditure that often follows excitement due to a new opportunity. During this Pre-Planning phase, confirm that the customers' needs are real and the solution is valid. There should be approval points throughout the pre-planning process during which the question is asked, "Do we have a solution to offer the customer(s) what they want and will pay for?"

Throughout the Opportunity Assessment and Pre-Planning phases a continued assessment of the cost and benefit of pursuing the objective should be made. The questions, "Is the opportunity real? Can we perform and win? Will the end result be worth it? Are the risks involved acceptable?" must be accurately addressed. The Pre-Planning phase ensures that all the essential homework is complete before the decision to continue assessing the opportunity is made.

Project Planning
The Project Planning phase should follow the approach developed in the Pre-Planning phase by meeting scheduled milestones for defining the product and manufacturing requirements, estimating costs and schedules, and , assessing risk, and mitigation planning. The project baseline clearly and concisely defines the cost, schedule, and technical performance of the project and product. This plan will be used to set up appropriate visibility, status and control mechanisms to support successful product development.

Implementation
Often started prior to any planning, the Implementation phase follows the approach formed in Project Planning by meeting scheduled milestones for product design and development, cost and schedule estimates, risk reduction, as well as managing changes to the plan. The success of the

efforts in this phase is almost entirely dependent on how well the project baseline is developed.

Ensure Technical Requirements are adequately and accurately defined.

Specification

A specification clearly defines the *performance* requirements of the product. It also defines features and functions. The Specification keeps the end in sight, and answers the question, "when is the product finished?" That is, the *acceptance* criteria, based on the *performance* requirements, should be well thought out and well defined. Acceptance tests for the design and sell-off are based on the specification. This significantly reduces feature-creep and rework time caused by chasing ever-changing requirements.

The technical requirements flow from customers' needs to operational requirements to functional requirements to design requirements to test requirements, or from vague ideas to specific ends. The path should be clear and accepted by all the parties involved. System requirements flow-down to supplier requirements, if any, should account for *reasonable* tolerance buildups, and system performance specifications should include *reasonable* performance margins to account for differences between prototypes (what's possible) and production units (what's probable).

Interface Control

An ICD (Interface Control Document) is necessary to address not only external interface requirements but also internal interface requirements. For instance, imbedded software, electrical, mechanical, inter-software and environmental interface requirements need to be defined. This minimizes feature creep by causing questions to be answered *early in the project*, and is especially useful to communicate interrelationships among design variables when several people are working on the project.

The result of this process is initiation of the Product Baseline. If performed correctly, this process will reduce the number of feature-creep-induced "fire-drills".

Ensure Resource Requirements are defined and satisfied.

Statement of Work
A SOW (Statement of Work) for both the Planning Phase and Product Development Phase should be developed. The Product Development SOW is based on the efforts required to meet the technical performance parameters defined in the specification, and is the basis for schedule and cost estimates. In this manner, costs and schedules are tied to the technical requirements in a clear and unambiguous manner.

Each SOW task specifies a responsible organization to perform the task, and assigns support organizations as required. Organizational involvement should be clearly identified so they may schedule the work appropriately. Each task should have dependencies described and results identified.

Work Breakdown Structure
A WBS (Work Breakdown Structure) greatly enhances the understanding of the total project's scope by defining the elements, which make up the product. Contrary to standard methods, a WBS which focuses on deliverables instead of

activities, which have already been defined in the SOW, provides the most acute insight into potential pitfalls. The WBS development *process* enables new perspectives to be fostered. This, in turn, allows a higher degree of risk identification, mitigation and preventative action planning.

Product Description

Develop a brief and uncomplicated Product Description. This Product Description aids in the communication of the baseline to all the team members. Although typically generated by engineering, it is not only a technical document. The job of the Product Description is to *support* understanding of the product being developed to all team members, and even customers.

The result of this process is the early evaluation of resource requirements, so assignments can be planned and commitments made, or corrective actions taken if the resources are not available.

Ensure key Milestones are Developed

Milestone Development

Identify key events from the start. This will allow for regular and periodic health checks of the project, and provide early warning signals of potential scheduling problems, so that *preventative* actions can be taken.

Operating Schedule Development

Tasks defined in the SOW for both the planning and project phases should have their schedule time estimated and dependencies defined. These scheduled times must also coincide with available or planned resources.

The schedules represent the task to be performed, so the technical performance parameters can be met. Thus, schedules can be tied to tasks, which are tied to performance. Key milestones are then folded into the operating schedules.

The result of this process is sufficiently detailed scheduling to support meaningful critical path assessments and provide for corrective and preventative action planning. From this, you can identify your "Top 10 Critical Paths" – then perform parametric analyses to get *ahead* of problems.

Develop Nonrecurring and Recurring Cost Estimates

Nonrecurring
Tasks defined in the SOW for both the planning and project phases should have their costs estimated by the organizations performing the tasks. These estimates are used to support cost and schedule estimates so that accurate trend analyses are developed.

Recurring
Life cycle costs not only include development costs but also production, packaging, shipping, procurement, maintenance and logistic support costs. These costs need to be identified early to ensure that *accurate* rates of return are calculated.

The result of this process is to place the team in a forward-looking mode, assessing the impacts of current decisions on future events.

Identify Key Risks

Risk Identification

Each project has some amount of risk associated with it. The purpose of taking the time to recognize major risks is to not only *identify* risks but also *mitigate* them. Options for dealing with these risks can then be developed. Costs and schedules can be identified with each risk so that senior management can make informed decisions as to the project risk level. These risks should be addressed at each major project review.

The result of this process is to make senior management aware of the potential risks associated with developing the proposed product.

As a "bonus" chapter...

How NOT to Manage Projects

Many clients have hired me to help them increase profits by improving their product development. Here are my secrets on how *not* to manage projects. By ignoring these seven critical product development areas, your company will better respond to the market and beat your competitors on price *and* schedule. (Make sure you copy this chapter and post it in a conspicuous place for all to avoid.)

1) **Never identify your customers' needs**: Whatever you do, don't waste time or energy to determine who your customers are, what they want or how they buy. By the time you've developed your product, their whimsical desires have changed anyway.

2) **Neglect your product's requirements**: As a corollary to the above, make sure never to discuss your product's features, functions nor performance. They are immaterial to what customers need. Besides, the marketing department will change what they want a few weeks into the project anyway. If you don't write the requirements down, then changes are *so* much easier.

3) **Ignore key project phases** and their relationships to development costs and revenue projections. They're too confusing to perform "what-if" analyses.

4) Don't define resource requirements: If you identify staffing needs or who you want on your project, you'll most assuredly tip your hand about who you think are exceptional performers. It's very difficult to steal resources from other projects if your staffing intentions are not written down for all to see. Keep them a secret.

5) Overlook key milestones and resultant operating schedules: If you haven't figured it out by now, let me say it straight – don't communicate your project's needs with anyone. If you think the schedule is tight now, wait until you state intangibles like milestones and due dates. And never tell your customers any of these dates – let them (and your competition) guess.

6) Never estimate nonrecurring and recurring costs: They'll just scare you.

7) Ignore key risks: Just let them happen to you; they're going to anyway. Why bother thinking about what can go wrong; you'll just stay up nights wishing you were blissful instead.

These are the many ways you can totally botch programs and projects, so that you become indispensable to your organization. Oh, and April Fools.

How to Define Products

According to a survey of the high-technology industry, 75 percent of the respondents stated that the area of product development that requires the <u>most</u> improvement in their companies is *better up-front planning and product definition.* **Seventy-five percent.**

In an industry that prides itself on innovation and technical leadership, it is amazing that the ability to plan for and define new products is lacking in so many companies. When senior managers of 20 software companies were asked about time-to-market, every one stated that product definition was a major problem. These same software development managers also stated they had no formal processes in place to alleviate this problem.

There is a burning desire to improve how customers' needs are translated not only into product requirements, but also to project definition and planning requirements. Since projects are the "transfer function" of product ideas to product reality, and since business performance is only as robust as the ability of a company to deliver high-quality products, it makes sense that high priority should be given to staffing product *and* project definition.

There are various ways to transfer customer needs to product requirements. One tool, which is gaining acceptance in a number of industries, is called QFD or Quality Function Deployment. Additionally, there are proven processes available to convert customer needs into specific design requirements (*product* definition), as well as cost, schedule, and risk estimates and planning (*project* definition). These processes involve translating customer needs into actions and tasks, which represent commitments by the performing organizations, partners and suppliers.

Flowing customer needs into directed company actions is no easy matter. It requires diligence by all involved with the project, including those in marketing, engineering, manufacturing, finance, procurement, employees, senior and middle management. Since the process is so complex, simplifying efforts must take place to boil complex issues down to easily understandable elements, and take seemingly disparate functions and break them into their common denominators.

In other words, translating requirements is a process. A process can be defined with inputs, outputs and efforts internal to the process. Improvements to the process can then be made as lessons learned and applied to subsequent projects.

There is no easy way to define products. There are, however, logical and methodical processes that can be applied and customized for each individual company. An important starting place to achieve success in product definition is to first determine the desired outcome of any improvements. Second, assess the status quo by reviewing current company processes. Third, review how current processes support the desired outcome. Fourth, determine the ideal situation for exceeding your customers' expectations. Last, cause the current situation to change to reflect the ideal situation, and the desired outcome.

Of course, this is just the beginning. As employees become more experienced in project definition, many more improvements to the entire process will be required, but by then making improvements will be much easier and the positive results from these improvements will be plain.

Note: Addendum 3 (www.synergy-usa.com/ESG-bonus.html) contains a Project Management glossary, to help you more accurately define products.

Solutions for this New Millennium

"Technology is getting ahead of our ability to manage it." This phrase summarizes the current situation in product development. Competitors seem to get products to market ever faster. Customers are better informed and demand more. How can you lead your company to successfully compete in these challenging times?

There are several areas for you to consider when leading your company to rapidly innovating new solutions, which fall into three major categories:

Organizational improvements:

Program management: Typically, technology companies delegate the program or project management function to Engineering or Marketing. Whenever a critical decision is required, Engineering will err on the side of technical correctness and Marketing will support the side of customer desires. This is just the way it is. Establishing a Program or Project Management group charged with responsibility for the Product Development (business profit and loss), and on par with Engineering and Marketing, results in the best decisions being made for the company overall. Referring to figure 1, you can see the integrative role Product Development has throughout the organization, when relating the internal workings of a company to the customer.

Venture Teams: An informal organization, responsible for company tactics and product strategies, enables the formal organization to rapidly integrate diverse perspectives into product development, achieving demanding corporate goals and objectives more rapidly. (Please see Addendum 2 at www.synergy-usa.com/ESG-bonus.html.)

Extended organization: In addition to the traditional organizational structure, consider your customers, Board of Directors, Board of Advisors, consultants, lawyers, accountants, bankers, educational institutions, and even the government as part of your team. Each has strengths to offer. Seek outside-the-box solutions to form a new integrated approach to product development.

Balanced strategic planning: In addition to top-led, annual strategic planning, ensure your detailed information gathering from all organizations affects your strategic direction on a day-to-day basis.

e-strategy: Technology can be leveraged to affect how you communicate internally and externally. Adapting and changing to get in front of your customers and ahead of your competition will enable your company to outperform itself. Organizations are traveling faster than the speed of information travel, making them supersonic in nature. The typical management controls become *inverse* at this organizational speed, so it is critical to increase the speed of information travel to compensate.

Virtual product development organization: In addition to the extended organization listed above, use others to virtually build your team to overcome more complex challenges.

Consider creating a Chief Knowledge Officer (CKO) position: The convergence of technology with ease of information access has created a quantum leap in our ability to move up the data-to-value continuum. (See page 147) The importance of this cannot be overstated: To compete in the coming years, companies will need to leapfrog their competition and lead customers toward their services. The CKO integrates financial information with operations information and market, and competitive information and provides executive's with the knowledge they need to make effective decisions.

Process improvements:

Product development process: Most organizations go straight from idea or concept into design and software coding, and feel they have a robust product development process. Inevitably the planning phase, where goals are turned into commitments, is left out. Planning is the single most critical part of a project's life. It is where requirements are defined, statements of work and specifications are developed, and organizational commitments are made. Although planning appears to add time into the schedule, it will significantly reduce time-to-market. The high-level process flow outlined in figure 2 shows the iterative nature of defining products and shifting from high-level goals to organizational commitment.

Imagination and creativity: Stress team-oriented problem solving by embracing the Seven New Management Tools. *"Planning for Quality, Productivity & Competitive Position"*[9] thoroughly discusses these tools. These are very powerful tools that dramatically improve organizational communication and speed information exchange.

Integrate customers into your requirements definition process: Learn about Quality Function Deployment (example, "Quality Function Deployment" – J.L. Bossert) and how it will enable your Marketing and Engineering departments to work with customers to define their wants and needs; as well as flowing these needs into your specifications, product requirements, and integration and test criteria.

Program Management methods: Once a senior executive responsible for the profit and loss aspects for each product line is in place, Engineering and Marketing will be free to do what they do best.

Twenty-first Century Imperatives:

Plan on commoditization: Work towards product and service differentiation, and figure out how to add value every step of the way. With price pressures always increasing, product and service differentiation is essential for competitive position.

Business-to-business- integration with your customers' processes: The more you enable your customers to outperform themselves, the more they will rely on your offerings and the more recurring revenue you will make. Also, the harder it will be for your competition to dislodge you.

Blur product and service offerings: Customers buy solutions. That is what excellent companies sell. Period.

Plan on disintermediation: Leverage the power of new technologies to enable your customers to make their own decisions about your products, then support them emphatically. (See www.chrome.com)

Make vs. buy: Use others' expertise as if it were your own. When in doubt, buy. The adage "stick to your knitting" should become a mantra, and following it will allow you to achieve far greater results.

Plan on mass-customization: If you can develop processes to deliver *customized* products for the same gross margin as mass-produced products, you will outperform your competition by orders of magnitude. (See www.dell.com)

In order to compete in the coming years, companies will have to adapt to the new (and ever-changing) economy, and in fact, become a leader in their specialty by re-defining themselves every step of the way. If you can integrate these ideas into your business model, you will be able to pull away from your competitors at break-neck speed.

Figure 1: In addition to the five core functions, others are needed as the company matures:

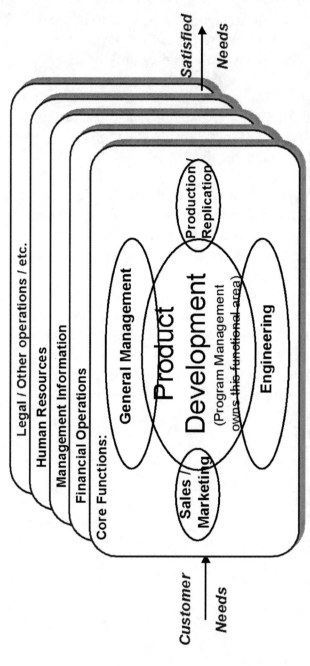

As long as you can view the company as an organism, as it grows, you will be able to integrate each new function so value is added. The core functions shown above are essential for satisfying customers as efficiently as possible.

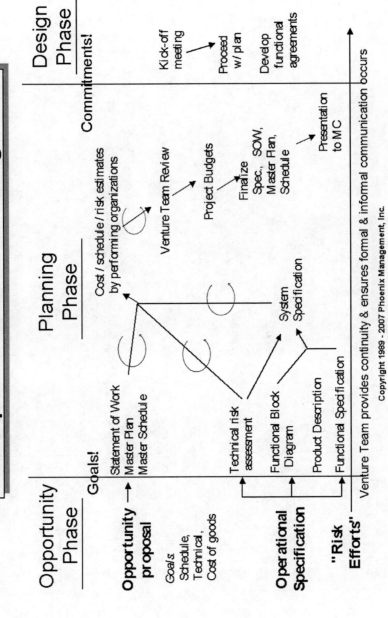

Figure 2: Details of Product Development Process - Planning Phase

Opportunity Phase

Goals!

Opportunity proposal

Goals
Schedule,
Technical,
Cost of goods

Statement of Work
Master Plan
Master Schedule

Technical risk assessment

Operational Specification

Functional Block Diagram

Product Description

Functional Specification

"Risk Efforts"

Planning Phase

Cost / schedule / risk estimates by performing organizations

System Specification

Venture Team Review

Project Budgets

Finalize Spec., SOW, Master Plan, Schedule

Presentation to MC

Design Phase

Commitments!

Kick-off meeting

Proceed w/ plan

Develop functional agreements

Venture Team provides continuity & ensures formal & informal communication occurs

Copyright 1989 - 2007 Phoenix Management, Inc.

169

Reasons Why Some Organizations Perform Poorly

As the company's leader, you want to win in your market. You want to beat your competitors and create value for your stockholders. However, there are many reasons why companies do not perform as well as possible. Even entrepreneurs of companies that are performing well look for ways to propel their companies to the next level. They also want to know what will trip them up. In either case, leaders need to see around corners to find the obstacles that will affect their companies' profitability, and do what is necessary to avoid these obstacles.

There are hundreds of reasons companies perform poorly or don't achieve their objectives. The following checklist outlines some of the major obstacles to a company's growth. Keep a lookout for these hazards as you plot your course.

Style
Organizational style starts at the top: lifestyle or high-growth, 9-to-5 or 16 hours a day...or somewhere in between. Assess your style to ensure it is in line with where you *want* your company to go.

✓ **Too stodgy:** If you have been in business for a while, and have tried unsuccessful change programs, chances are neither your managers nor employees are going to be too open to new changes. Improvement cannot happen without change.

✓ **Too entrepreneurial:** The management of many dot.com companies represents the flip side of being too stodgy. Moving fast is great, but many new entrepreneurs have never had responsibility for making a profit. It is very easy to spend money and extremely difficult to sell profitably. So make sure your team has a number of seasoned veterans from the profit wars.

Organizational Maturity

Too often companies led by founders are built around their particular area of expertise. Assess your company's strength as you would potential employees' to see if there is balance.

✓ **Too "techie:"** Great engineers may not make great entrepreneurs. The company can get analysis paralysis, with insufficient emphasis on marketing and sales. It is very difficult to break above $5 million in sales with this culture. Usually the voice of technology is considered without regard to what products and services customers will pay for in the future.

✓ **Too "salesy:"** Entrepreneurs who have sales backgrounds may not fully understand the reality of technology development. Often, it is difficult to appreciate what it takes to actually make a product. Frequently, the company reaches a revenue limit before running into difficult financial times. Usually the voice of marketing is considered, without regard to technical requirements.

✓ **Organizational imbalance:** Whether a strong technical leader or a strong sales leader runs the company, the result of not having a balanced organization is the same: limited growth, chaotic communication, and lack of internal alignment.

✓ **Lack of project management:** Project management (PM) *software* does not equal project management. It requires [1] an organization that embraces the discipline of PM, [2] the right PM processes in place, that are understood and followed, and [3] people skilled in the processes, with their PM manager reporting to the CEO. Period. Without this discipline in place, the voice of business is not addressed, at the expense of lasting profits.

✓ **No recognized informal organizations:** Informal organizations exist. Sometimes, entrepreneurs choose to ignore them. By having and acknowledging temporary teams, companies can dramatically improve their operational and project performance. (Examples are Venture Teams and Core Teams.)

✓ **Management immaturity:** Too often, managers who have been with a small company their entire career don't realize what professional management really entails. One entrepreneur recently told me, *"People who have spent at least 5 to10 years in large corporations and then worked in small companies are far better equipped to lead a company to stellar performance."* Typically, these people have seen all the functions that a large company requires to grow. They recognize when the company needs these functions; and they recognize the roles, responsibilities and relationships necessary for a company to be successful

Internal Systems

Excellent companies sometimes position themselves for failure by not having the proper systems in place to deal with their next level of growth.

✓ **Inefficient information systems:** These days, organizations are turning on their heads. It used to be that the company's leader generally had more information than anyone else, and could make decisions based on that inequality. Now, employees have more and better access to information and the leader must rely on the employees, who need to be empowered to access and act on this information.

✓ **Process immaturity:** In addition to information systems, lack of an organizational system (or critical internal processes) is often the cause of a company tripping up. For instance, companies trying to embrace the web can only integrate this technology by web-enabling their internal processes. No processes, no web-enablement.

Planning Maturity
No one can predict the future, but companies that plan for risk are able to take on even more risk.

✓ **Lack of Strategy:** If you're too busy dealing with day-to-day issues, chances are you're not able to think strategically, let alone act strategically. This is typically caused by organizational and/or process immaturity. Many companies don't really know how to conduct a true strategic planning session. They only focus on quarterly goals, which is a terrible use of management's time.

✓ **No business plan:** Not having a business plan, no matter how simple, is a cause for many business failures. The simpler the business, products, or services, the simpler the plan can be. If the company has a strategic plan, that may suffice.

✓ **Unchanging business plan:** Some companies spend so much time developing a business plan they don't want to vary from it, even when the market or economy changes. Although not nearly as prevalent a problem, this behavior can dramatically reduce a company's performance.

✓ **No project planning:** Businesses are only as successful as their product (or service) lines. Product lines are only as successful as individual products within the line, and products are only as successful as individual projects. No project planning means a much higher probability of failure. Requirements can be ill defined, with true cost and schedule estimates missing, so that goals are not converted into commitments.

Business Maturity
Entrepreneurs who accept that tough business decisions are required for their company to be successful are more comfortable making these decisions.

✓ **Poor cash management:** When you run out of cash, nothing else matters. That said, penny-wise risk-averse companies prolong their suffering.

With a strategic or business plan, you should know your company's direction. Any money spent should be in helping the company achieve stated and agreed-to goals and objectives.

✓ **Inability to niche:** An important question to ask is "What is your preferred customer profile?" Companies without the answer perform much worse than companies with entrepreneurs who do. Simple as that.

Leadership
The most important element to success is the person leading the company. Leader defines the company in foundational ways. There are many reasons companies perform poorly, but they always come down to leadership. Here are just a few ideas for you to ponder.

✓ **No clear vision:** If you don't have a strategic plan, then have clear core values, a vision and a mission. And then communicate these values throughout the company. The CEO's role is to [1] have the vision, [2] share the vision, [3] get resources, and [4] get out of the way. No vision equals misspent resources, which lead to failed projects and failed organizations.

✓ **Autocratic:** CEOs certainly must lead. entrepreneurs typically have an acceptance of risk far greater than anyone else in the company. CEO characteristics are well known (cut to the chase, damn the torpedoes, etc.). However, in order to lead a company to greatness, successful CEOs empower their people to have the authority to make decisions. They also have an organization that is mature enough to allow, and have integrated systems to enable this empowerment.

✓ **Laissez Faire:** The flip side to an autocratic leader is one who randomly lucks into success. These entrepreneurs can build companies, but they typically cannot lead them to greatness. Again, balance is necessary, and a true self-assessment can help.

Change is Essential to Survival
The common thread throughout these important points is change. In today's business climate, with rapidly changing technological shifts in the very way we live and work, a company that cannot change is a company that will not survive.

Why is it so hard for people to change? *"Change dishonors your past.*[10]*"* This is true for people, and it is also true for companies. If you recognize your own unwillingness to change, and deal with it, the people in your company will follow your example, and the changes necessary for success can occur.

Acknowledgements - General

The author would like to thank the following people:

Sylvia Waack has been there throughout - when I was in large companies, one-person start-ups and everywhere in between. She really is the true inspiration of my life. To say any more would be to say less.

Nicole, Nathan and Michael have put up with my incessant discussions on the similarities between the family organism and business organization. They have also taught me quite a bit about leadership and the human side of leadership.

Brad Paul is a super brother – we've talked about what makes great managers, and what companies need to do to become more professional… to build value for all stakeholders.

Robert Campbell has been a true friend over the past 30⁺ years. He's provided sage advice and counsel on how to start and grow businesses, even when I was considering my first entrepreneurial venture in 1978. He also plays a mean guitar lead now and then.

William Campbell has been an entrepreneur's advocate for a long time. He is a brilliant man who can see around corners and has significant insights for such a young man. He has been gracious with his time and has helped me on numerous occasions - providing guidance for several start-up ideas.

Wayne Embree has likewise been extremely helpful and provided unique and valuable insights and perspective.

Les Fahey has likewise been very helpful and pointed me and my clients in the right direction, time and again. He has also been very helpful to our consulting firm on time after time.

Larry Hughes has provided support and wisdom well beyond his years. He helped guide me from the "coal" I once was – his friendship will always be treasured.

Steve Jaynes "gets it" on so many levels. He has been a real inspiration for me over the years. He has also provided me invaluable advice and counsel on so many subjects.

Ross Macdonald has provided unending help and support over the past twenty years. He has been a true friend and believer. We have been through the dark times together as well as been part of the roller coaster that is the new e-conomy. He's provided me with sound advice and counsel on too many occasions to recall, usually over some great northwest ale. Thank you for all your help.

Virginia Mort is one of the most positive people I know. She encouraged me to do my best and taught me a lot about the finer aspects of leadership.

Richard Odum was the most influential mentor of my career. By his actions, he provided a definition of what true leadership means. He is a role model few have had the pleasure of knowing. He had an immense impact on my learning, management style, outlook on business, working with people and general business acumen. Without him as a guide and mentor, I would not have been as successful as I have.

Margo Parker showed me what a professionally run HR organization can do for a company, and especially for individuals' careers in helping a company.

Mike Peron has been a great friend over the past 30[+] years. His management and leadership styles helped shape who I am today.

Pat Quinn and I have had many discussions, usually on Tuesday evening about the nature of entrepreneurship, personal behavior, and just plain *being*.

Michael Shenker once saved my life. He has shown me the Zen side of consulting, and has provided different thinking on many levels.

Greg and **Tracey Warnke** have also been great friends - with us through life's and pizza's thick and thin. Good times.

Patrick Wheeler has helped me in all things financial. He's been an exceptional partner in our firm, Synergy Consulting Group, LLC, and provided advice on client matters, and has always followed through with whatever he says he will do. His ethics are beyond reproach – together we have provided truly synergistic value to our clients.

Eric Pozzo and **Debi Coleman** were very gracious in writing the Forwards and provided excellent feedback. Thank you.

There are several others who I have learned a great deal from: Dean Baker, Ed Benthale, Joe Berg, Steve Bonkowski, Ed Clark, Don Eakin, Dick Ekstrom, Tom Godfrey, Richard Lindberg, Frank McNabb, Frank Reyes, Tom Sneed, and Joe Stopper to name a few. Also – to the first real entrepreneur I met, Gene Kinsel (Kinsel Landscaping); the person who promoted me to manager for the first time, at age 19 – Zim Troutt (Rainbow Sandals), and of course, my 9th grade English teacher in Las Vegas, NV, – Mrs. Fulton.

Acknowledgements

The author would like to thank several people and organizations:

Larry Wade, previously at the **Software Association of Oregon** supported the initial concept of a series of monthly articles aimed at helping entrepreneurs improve their companies. Having written many business plans – and reviewed even more – through the **Oregon Entrepreneur's Forum (now Network)** provided the impetus to address recurring issues entrepreneurs face in building their companies. Based on the response to these monthly articles, several associations across the United States published most of the articles found in this handbook, including the **Software Development Forum, Software Council of Southern California, Indiana Information Technology Association, and North East Ohio Software Association**.

And for helping to add to or review chapters in this handbook:

(1) **What are the Core Values of Leading CEOs?** The author would like to acknowledge the American Electronics Association, Oregon Council. The information was gathered while part of the AEA's Partnership for Competitiveness Committee's efforts to support the CEOs of AEA member firms. (Now TechAmerica)

(2) **Building Your Team:** Mr. Eric Pozzo contributed to this chapter in the area of the roles and responsibilities of the Board of Directors (sidebar). Eric is Vice President of Operations at First Silicon Solutions, Inc. and has been a member of the Board of Directors for ABC Technologies for five years.

(3) **Creating Your Stock Structure:** Mr. Les Fahey, previous partner at KPMG in Portland, Oregon reviewed this chapter and the associated spreadsheet on corporate structure.

(4) Raising Money in a Tight Market: Gerry Langeler is a Partner at OVP Venture Partners. Kevin Gabelein is Managing Director at Fluke Venture Partners in Bellevue, Washington. Robert Campbell is Managing Director at B | Riley - an investment banking firm in Orange County, California. Wayne Embree is Managing Partner at Reference Capital in Portland, Oregon.

(5) The Realities of Raising Money: Mr. Alan Dishlip was General Partner at Utah Venture Partners (now Pelion). He is now at SingleCLick. Mr. Bill Kallman is Managing Partner with Timberline Ventures (www.timberlinevc.com), an Oregon information technology venture firm. Ms. Nancy Isely-Fletcher was with Coldstream Capital (www.coldstream.com), in Seattle, Washington.

(6) Organizing for the Customer: *Critical Path to Corporate Renewal*, Beer, Eisenstat and Spector; Harvard Business School Press; 1990 ISBN 0-87584-239-9

(7) A Simple Secret to Successful Leadership / The Real Value of Market Research: Mr. Michael Shenker for his insight into motivating factors and his highly quotable quote.

(8) How to Hire the Best: Ms. Pamela Jones, Principal of JONES AND JONES, a technology search firm, Mr. Dave Opton, Executive Director of Exec-U-Net, a networking enabler, Ms. Kathy Holmquist, a human resources consultant, Mr. Frank Moscow, President of The Brentwood Group, Ltd., a Pacific Northwest executive search firm,

(9) How to Predict the Future: Decisioneering, makers of *Crystal Ball*, 303-534-1515.

(10) Solutions for the New Mellinnium / What's your e-strategy?: *Planning for Quality, Productivity & Competitive Position;* – H.S. Gitlow; Dow Jones-Irwin, 1990; ISBN 1-55623-357-4

(11) Reasons why some organizations perform poorly: Mr. William Lewis, Portland, Oregon based lawyer.

(12) Change or Fail. Mr. Rene Fritz is an entrepreneur and leads a group of CEOs in the Vancouver, Washington area. He can be reached at rfritz@ceforum.com.

(13) All chapters: Ms. Alexandra Prentiss edited all chapters and Andrew Rowe and Pat Quinn's reviews helped morph the entire project. Thank you.

(14) Cover: Mr. Bob Bredemeier created the artwork. He can be reached through: www.bobbredemeier.com.

About the author

Mark Paul has over thirty years of business and leadership experience in bootstrapped start-ups through Global 500 corporations, in consulting, executive and interim executive roles. He is a Managing Partner at **Synergy Consulting Group** (www.synergy-usa.com). He's been an interim Chief Operating Officer at a software company, where he led the company to dramatic improvements: 67% improvement in sales, nearly 10x cash improvement, developed 8x new products and significant increase in profits – in less than two years – transforming them into a web-based company, with a profitable business model (in 1996); and interim President of an "Internet company", CEO of a public telecom company, and Chief Marketing Officer of a $34 million manufacturing company, increasing DM rates from under 2% to nearly 9%, reducing customer-acquisition costs by 62% and generating over $6 million in lifetime value – in less than 12 months . He's dramatically increased shareholder value for many companies, located funding and helped more than a few people become millionaires.

Prior to consulting, Mark spent eleven years at Ford and Northrop Corporations. He was a senior executive at Northrop Corporation; building a multi-million dollar business unit in two years, where he led up to 250 people in "line" and project roles. He was awarded U.S. Patent # 4,631,583, for a software-controlled electro-optical device, has a degree in Physics from the University of California, Irvine, post-graduate studies in technology management at Cal-Tech, and has board-level experience. In his spare time, he plays guitar, and has produced two CDs (*Lonesome Taxi* and *aphasia* [www.aphasia-music.com]). He is particularly interested in renewable energy (www.NXergy.com), international business and the music instrument business. His wife of 33 years and three children are his reasons for living. He can be reached by visiting his website at www.synergy-usa.com.

What readers said about the 1st & 2nd editions of the book

What readers of the first two editions say:

"The Entrepreneur's Survival Guide is a clear guide for the processes and hurdles we will encounter in the future as we move toward being an established business."
John Friess, VP of Marketing at Wired.MD and founder of StarveUps.

"Great book. Just wanted to tell you that I read your book and was quite impressed. I can understand now why everyone wanted me to read it. I think it will be very helpful for me."
Nate von Colditz, Founder & President, e-Ference, Inc.

"Having been a Marketing Communications Manager for 6 ½ years and also in high tech sales.... what you say rings true."
Don Somppi – was General Manager of Logical (PSSG)

"Just a short note to thank you. I enjoyed it very much and have taken it to heart. I am the founder and CEO of a new start-up, and this is my third go-round. Your message is… oh so true, and I intend to apply it all."
Alexandra Saunders – is founder & CEO of ExtremeNature.com

"Hard-hitting and sage advice throughout. Great model. I really want this in the hands of my students. I need 30 copies."
Dr. Aaron Johnson – Professor, Oregon Sate University, Food Innovation Center

"We're deep in the process of strategic planning here at Timberline - great timing."
Thomas Coleman - Product Development, Senior VP, Timberline Software

"I'm becoming ever more cognizant of the value in focusing more and more on many of the leadership items you mention. You provide some excellent information, both practical and 'usable'. Just wanted to send you a note and say thanks."
Greg Ross - IT Division Manager, Employment Trends, Inc.

Additional products and services to help your business grow

Available at www.synergy-usa.com/newproducts.html:

How to Attract More Customers... in good times & bad:
Book & Audio CD

Do you have all the customers you need? Are you looking for cost-effective ways to attract more "A" customers? Have you tried trade shows, advertisements, newsletters, direct mail, PR, telesales, brochures, and dozens of other ways...without the success you would like? Are your sales & marketing efforts both consistent and producing results / ROI you want? Learn how you can turbo-charge your marketing and sales efforts, without paying a fortune.

How Entrepreneurs can Survive & Thrive in Challenging Times.
This live audio CD captures Mark Paul's kick-off presentation for Oregon Graduate Institute's Center for Technology Entrepreneurship, and includes examples and encouragement for entrepreneurs.

Funding / growth Spreadsheet / Template: Excel Spreadsheet

Entrepreneurs ask me all the time: "How much of the company should I 'sell,' for how much money?" And: "How can I maintain my equity as more investors capitalize the company?"

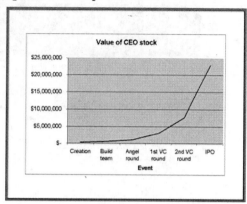

This spreadsheet template answers those questions, & more. It is highlighted in the Entrepreneur's Survival Guide, but the actual template provides you an interactive way to "plug & chug" your own numbers. That way, you can integrate your management organization (& the options you'll need to share), & have it tie directly into the main spreadsheet.

Synergy's Customer-attraction Quotient[tm] Assessment & Report: This assessment and report will quantify your ability to attract more customers. By answering a brief survey, you will receive a customized report with actionable customer-attraction recommendations.

Why should you take this? > If you need more customers, this will pinpoint areas needing improvement. > If you are looking for the most cost-effective use of your limited dollars.

What will you learn? > A customized assessment of your customer-attraction capabilities. > A comparison of your answers relative to best-in-class companies. > A comparison of your answers relative to all respondents. > Specific recommendations & actions you can take in over a dozen areas.